CATCHING THE VISION

Val Fotherby teaches history at a large comprehensive school. She gained her BA degree in Economic and Social History and her MPhil degree as a mature student. Val is married to David, President of the North Humberside chapter of the FGBMFI and Field Representative in the North East.

Catching the Vision

VAL FOTHERBY

KINGSWAY PUBLICATIONS
EASTBOURNE

First published 1989

Front cover design by W James Hammond

British Library Cataloguing in Publication Data

Fotherby, Val
Catching the vision
1. Great Britain. Christian businessmen's organisations. Full Gospel Businessmen's Fellowship, history
I. Title
267'.13

ISBN 0-86065-704-3

Production and printing in Great Britain for
KINGSWAY PUBLICATIONS LTD
Lottbridge Drove, Eastbourne, East Sussex BN23 6NT by
Nuprint Ltd, 30b Station Road, Harpenden, Herts AL5 4SE

Contents

Acknowledgements

I would like to thank all those people who have helped me in the writing of this book. Because they are so many it would be impossible to name each one. However, I would particularly like to acknowledge the following people.

Walter Wainwright, my uncle, who died suddenly in January 1988, for it was he who first told us about the FGBMFI. Alistair and Sylvia Humphreys who gave us a copy of *The Happiest People On Earth* and took us to our first breakfast meeting. Pauline Sture for checking the early chapters of the manuscript. The International Directors of the Fellowship in the United Kingdom and Ireland: Bob Spilman, Allan Jones, Bert Sture, Jim Winter, Don Latham, Dillon Harris, Hector Crory, Buzz Dulley and John Wright. The many Field Representatives, Presidents of chapters, members and associates of the Fellowship who gave their time to be interviewed.

I would also like to thank all those who gave David and myself such wonderful hospitality in our 6,000 miles of travel to obtain the information and stories which make up this book.

Lastly I would like to thank David, my husband, whose idea it was and who has encouraged, and criticised when necessary, throughout the whole project. And our daughter Jane who has put up with our absences and my many hours on the word processor!

Foreword

On our most recent visit to the United Kingdom, in 1988, we visited a dozen chapters of the Full Gospel Business Men's Fellowship over a period of four months. On each occasion we came away impressed.

Impressed, first of all, by the quality of the worship—the dignified, very British, quiet enthusiasm for the message of the Gospel. Impressed, too, by the fullness of that Gospel, including prayers for people in need of a new beginning, prayers for baptism in the Holy Spirit, prayers for the sick in body and in heart.

Impressed by the continual emphasis on the church (the local churches of varying denominations) as the body of Christ, and the Fellowship as a service to, never a substitute for, that church.

As at any time when people are being helped and healed and inspired, there's a story behind it. The story of a struggle.

In November 1965, some 400 members of the Fellowship from chapters all over North America flew to London to encourage the start of a similar laymen's ministry in the UK. We arrived with our ten-gallon hats, our loud ties and polyester suits to be greeted with amusement by the press but with surprising openness by the British public. Men in the United Kingdom and Ireland were ready to listen to other men—businessmen, professional men, men who worked with their hands—proclaiming a Gospel filled with power. Chapters sprang up everywhere.

Only to wither and die. At least, so it seemed.

In her fast-paced book *Catching the Vision*, Val Fotherby traces the various strands of the story after that initial airlift of 1965. She follows the hopeful beginnings of a Full Gospel Business Men's outreach in Britain. The failure of the chapters to hold on to the imported vision. The rekindling of the fire as the British Fellowship found its own identity, its own way of expressing itself, while never compromising the essential purpose of the FGBMF International—to bring men and women to Jesus.

The Fellowship has more than 250 chapters in Britain now. As the work expands and multiplies, people everywhere will be grateful for Val Fotherby's meticulously researched narrative. Not because it is the story of an organisation, but because it is an account of God at work at this time in this place.

JOHN AND ELIZABETH SHERRILL

Introduction

Saturday 20th November, 1965. In the lobby of the Los Angeles International Airport, about 1,000 people are gathered together. They are there to send off with prayer and blessings some 130 of their friends and families. Among these are well-known figures such as Nicky Cruz and Demos and Rose Shakarian. On the runway stands a Scandinavian Airways jet, its destination London.

This is a unique happening. The electrifying presence of God is sensed by everyone. Five ex-drug addicts sing, 'We've come this far by faith'; other men stand up and speak about the miracles that have allowed them to be part of this historic event.

On the same day many hundreds of miles away in the North East, another group is gathered at Kennedy International Airport, New York, awaiting the arrival of Judge Kermit Bradford. He has been delayed by court cases and bad weather in Atlanta. With only minutes to spare his helicopter crosses the Hudson from Newark, New Jersey, and he joins the other 143 people boarding the plane in the darkness of this early winter evening. Included in this group are the well-known writer John Sherrill, preacher and presenter of '700 Club', Pat

Robertson, and author Harold Hill. Only just visible along one side of the jet are the words 'First Over the Pole'. Its destination on this flight—London.

Chicago is the departure point for yet a third jet. Here, as in Los Angeles, the 127 people boarding are sent off with songs and prayers by a host of well wishers. Among this group are the Rev Derek Prince and his wife, and Steve Shakarian whose father has already left from Los Angeles. As their jet lifts off everyone on board shouts, 'Praise the Lord!' Destination for this flight—London.

I

The Armenian Connection

What should they take with them? Only those possessions the family could carry on their back, he decided, the rest must be sold for whatever money they could get. In his own load he would carry the heavy wood-burning brass samovar, a tangible link with the old way of life. The farm had been sold, their papers were in order, it was time to go.

For the Shakarian family of Kara Kala in Armenia, 1905 was the year of their 'exodus'. Five years had passed since the first of their friends and neighbours had left for the American continent, and now Grandfather Demos was to follow in their footsteps. The journey would be long, expensive and more than a little difficult with a wife, six daughters, a thirteen-year-old son, plus their remaining worldly possessions. Such decisions were not undertaken lightly. Tragic events had caused families like the Shakarians to take this monumental step.

Armenians are an Indo-European people with a highly distinctive culture. They embraced Christianity late in the third century. Their native land has now been absorbed into North-eastern Turkey and the Armenian Soviet Socialist Republic. As part of the Ottoman Empire until

1918, they suffered a great deal at the hands of the Turkish Moslems. Six thousand Armenians were murdered on the streets of Constantinople by a Turkish mob in 1896, and in the following years nearly two million died in massacres and forced marches.

But this Armenian family did not leave their native land because of massacre or forced march, but because of a word from God himself. In 1900 a band of travelling Russian Christians came to Kara Kala. At one of their meetings they prayed with Grandfather Demos, laying their hands on his head. He burst into joyous prayer, not in his native tongue but in a language he had never learned. Grandfather Demos had experienced the baptism in the Holy Spirit.

Following this experience he began to believe certain prophetic messages that had been given to the people of his village. One of these was particularly remarkable. About the middle of the nineteenth century, a boy of eleven called Efim who had an amazing capacity for prayer spent seven days praying and fasting. During that time God gave him a vision in which he saw charts and a message in beautiful handwriting. He asked for pen and paper and copied every shape and diagram that came in the vision. What was extraordinary was that this boy could not then, or later, read or write. The message declared that in future days all Christians would be in danger of their lives and that unless everyone in the region fled they would be brutally murdered. Through the maps copied by the young boy, God clearly directed his faithful to go and settle on the West coast of the United States of America.

In 1905 God spoke again through Efim, announcing that the time had come when the vision would be fulfilled. Grandfather Demos and many others had no hesitation in acting upon God's word. They sold their possessions and set out in faith.

The early years were very hard. All the money from the sale of the farm had been used to finance their journey, and jobs were not easy to find in America. The death of Grandfather Demos only a year after their arrival left his son, Isaac, as head of the family at the age of fourteen. Again, it was a word from God that gave direction for the future. God spoke through Deuteronomy (chapter 28 verses 3 to 8) concerning his blessings on his people and on the land. Isaac believed this word for himself and by the time he was twenty not only was he able to buy arable land and three milk cows, but he was also able to marry the beautiful young daughter of another Armenian family, Zarouhi Yessayian. God blessed them both, and on 21st July 1913 their first child was born. They called him Demos, after his Grandfather.

From the time of their arrival in California, the Armenian Pentecostals always met together on Sunday afternoons in the front room of the Shakarian home in Boston Street, Los Angeles. As their numbers grew, a small church building was constructed on Gless Street. Jesus was at the centre of their lives and they brought up their children to know and love him. Young Demos was no exception. He knew Jesus as a close friend from a very early age and loved to talk to him while working in the fields.

When he was ten Demos broke his nose. It did not heal correctly, leaving the ear canal and nasal passages blocked. Eventually this resulted in acute deafness which the doctor was unable to cure in spite of several operations. But Demos harboured no resentment, only a belief that Jesus could heal him in a miraculous way.

One Sunday morning in 1926, Demos experienced a strange but pleasant feeling as he prepared for church. This was always the highlight of the week and his three younger sisters were chattering excitedly, but Demos was unable to participate because of his deafness. There was a tremendous expectancy in the air as the Armenian congregation gathered, for God had been doing wonderful things among them. As the service progressed Demos experienced a warm sensation as if someone was putting a heavy woollen blanket over his shoulders, but looking round he couldn't see anyone touching him. He was filled with longing to tell Jesus how much he loved him and, like Grandfather Demos, he began to speak in a language he did not know.

Many hours later in his room at home, still very much aware of the Lord's presence, he heard Jesus speaking to him. Three times the Lord asked him if he would ever doubt his power, and three times Demos answered, 'No, Lord Jesus.' Those in church that day had been thrilled to see Demos being 'baptised in the Holy Spirit', none more so than his parents. The next morning, however, brought further excitement when Demos realised that for the first time in three years he could hear. Realising his healing was for a purpose, he asked the Lord to show him the work he wanted him to do.

Over the next few years the Shakarian family prospered, eventually owning the largest dairy herd in California. Their business even flourished throughout the depression and they began to cherish dreams of owning the biggest herd in the world! But Demos had other dreams on his mind. By 1932 he had already chosen the woman he wished to marry. She was called Rose. Being an obedient son he followed the Armenian tradition in which the parents would meet and consult before giving their consent. This tradition also forbade any contact between the young couple until the official engagement. Demos had mentally prepared speeches over and over again, but when the time came, his first words to Rose were that he knew God wanted them together. To his amazement she told him that she had always prayed that those would be the first words spoken to her by the man she was to marry!

Part of the prophecy given back in Kara Kala had promised that God would bless and prosper them, but there was more. God also promised that, like Abraham, he would cause their seed to be a blessing to the nations. As Demos saw the first part being fulfilled in the early years of his marriage, he began to wonder about the second. Was God asking them to do something more than just being good employers and generally helpful in the community? He began to pray regularly that once again the Lord would show him the direction he was to go.

Faithful to his word, God spoke clearly to Demos in a vision. He showed him a large park where their family often went for picnics. Many people were sitting on the grass and in the middle there was a large platform which he climbed onto and began to tell the people about Jesus. Amazingly, God had given the same vision to Rose. However, one aspect of the vision troubled Demos—he found it very difficult to speak out in public. But such was his faith and love for Jesus that some weeks later he found himself standing in the open air in front of a crowd with a microphone in a somewhat clammy hand. Surely all those sermons he had listened to would enable him to speak that afternoon. Many readers will sympathise with Demos as he struggled to tell the people of his neighbourhood about Jesus. After some time a man near the platform began to weep. He said that Demos' words were true and that God had been very good to him as well. Taking the microphone from Demos, he began to tell the crowd his story. He was followed by another, and by the end of that afternoon six people had committed themselves to following Jesus.

This one meeting set the pattern not just for local evangelism but eventually for city-wide campaigns. Demos, very much aware that he was not a speaker, began to realise that God had called him to be a helper. His role was to organise these campaigns, which often lasted a number of weeks, and bring in well-known speakers. He also encouraged pastors from all denominations to work and pray together. At the end of the campaign people who had made a commitment to Jesus would be shared among the denominations so that every church benefited.

It was not until many years later, during meetings in the summer of 1944, that Demos realised something that had remained vaguely at the back of his mind for a long time. As an Armenian, he was used to a male-dominated church. Not only were men the decision makers in the church, but they would also be present at every meeting. Over the years, however, Demos had increasingly noticed that the congregations at the meetings he organised were predominantly female. In fact, the ratio seemed to be about ten women to one man. He asked his close friend, Dr Charles Price, if all the men in the Los Angeles area were overseas. Somewhat puzzled at the question, Price replied that there had never been so many men in the area. When Demos gave the reason for his question, Price laughed at his friend's naïvety, explaining to this very Armenian man that American men did not consider Christianity to be compatible with masculinity. In America, apart from the clergy, women were the church.

The two friends discussed this issue many times, trying to figure out exactly why successful American businessmen in particular were rarely found inside a church. Charles confessed to Demos that when such men came to talk to him he couldn't understand their language and their concerns were remote from his thinking. However, one statement he made was to stick in Demos' mind. It concerned the outpouring of God's blessings in the last days.

'Demos,' he said, 'I will not be here to see it, but you will witness one of the major events foretold in the Bible. Just before Jesus returns to the earth God's Spirit is going to descend on all flesh, and laymen—ordinary men and women, people in shops and factories—will be the most important channel through whom he will work.'

Over the next seven years Demos continued to organise meetings, the scale of these increasing. In 1951 he helped set up a series of meetings for Oral Roberts in Los Angeles. These were the biggest he had ever been involved with—approximately 200,000 people over 16 days. After the campaign, Demos explained to Oral that in spite of the obvious success of such meetings he felt that God was calling him to something different. When Oral questioned him, Demos shared his vision for a ministry that would encourage businessmen to tell other businessmen about their experience of God. They would not preach but simply talk in a very natural way about what God had done in their lives. He envisaged salesmen coming to listen to a man because he too was a salesman, and likewise dentists, plumbers and so on, each speaking to men on their own level.

Demos had even settled on the name of the group: Full Gospel Business Men's Fellowship International. The title seemed a little cumbersome, but Demos explained why he had chosen it. '*Full Gospel*' meant that one could share freely about everything in the Bible, whether healing, tongues or deliverance. '*Business Men*' implied ordinary laymen. '*Fellowship*' described a coming together of equals outside a church setting. And '*International*' expressed what Demos felt God was saying about the scope of the work. Demos smiled as he explained the last word. But Oral Roberts didn't, for he could see God's hand in this work.

When Demos asked him if he would come and speak to a group of businessmen in Los Angeles, he readily agreed. The venue was Clifton's Cafeteria, well known and always busy during the week. Demos was determined to give God every assistance and he rang all the Spirit-filled businessmen he could think of to invite them along. He could scarcely contain his excitement that October morning, fully expecting to find the room full. The scene that met his eyes could scarcely have been further from those expectations. As Demos, Rose and Oral walked in there were only eighteen men. Nevertheless, at the end of his twenty-minute talk Oral prayed that the Fellowship would grow in the strength of the Lord Jesus alone and that he would send it marching in power across America and around the world.

The following year was one of disappointment and frustration. Demos spent thousands of dollars travelling and promoting the Fellowship, but not a single contribution was made and no other groups, or 'chapters' as he was to call them, were started. How could he have got it so wrong? He had been so certain that this was what God wanted him to do. There was nothing else to do but close the chapter and dissolve the Fellowship. God, however, had very different plans.

Saturday 29th December was to be the last breakfast of the Fellowship. Over their evening meal on the preceding evening, Demos, Rose and their guest, evangelist Tommy Hicks, discussed the situation. Tommy, a good friend, understood the anguish Demos was going through and tried to encourage him. That night, knowing he would be unable to sleep, Demos told the other two to go to bed and decided to go into the living room and stay there in prayer until he had heard from the Lord. It was to be the most remarkable night of his life.

Falling prostrate on the floor, Demos wept and prayed in tongues. Then he heard the same voice which had spoken to him at the age of thirteen, 'Demos, will you ever doubt my power?' He stayed in that position until three o'clock in the morning when Rose, also unable to sleep, came to join him. She sat down at the organ and began to play quietly. Then, as the music filled the room,

Demos saw the ceiling apparently recede to be replaced by a daytime sky. At that moment Rose stopped playing and began to speak in tongues, afterwards giving the interpretation: 'My Son, I knew you before you were born. I have guided you every step of the way. Now I am going to show you the purpose of your life.'

While hearing her words, Demos felt as if he was leaving his body although he was actually still on his knees. He rose higher and higher above the earth until he could see the whole of the United States from the West to the East.

What he saw terrified him. His eyes focused on millions of men standing shoulder to shoulder, yet cut off from one another and lifeless, their eyes staring straight ahead, unblinking and unseeing. But the vision did not stop there. The earth began to turn slowly, and he saw the different continents of South America, Africa and Asia. Yet again he saw startling close-ups of brown, black and white faces, each one wretched and lifeless.

Completely unaware of what Demos was seeing, Rose began to speak again: 'My son, what you see next is going to happen very soon.'

For a second time Demos saw the earth revolve, but what a difference! The scene was no longer of death but life. The faces were transformed, their eyes shining with joy. Heads were lifted up and hands raised towards heaven. Men had been brought out of their prison of isolation and were now joined together by love.

Slowly, Demos felt himself returning to earth and his own living room with Rose seated at the organ. Looking at his watch as he got up somewhat stiffly from his knees, he realised that it was half past three in the morning. Sharing what he had seen with Rose, they both knew that the Lord was telling them to go on with the Fellowship and that he would use it to fulfil the vision. As they passed Tommy's door on their way to bed, he called out to them.

He was still wearing his suit, lying face downwards on the floor, supporting Demos as best he knew how—in prayer. Tommy wanted to know what had been happening because he had experienced, as never before in his life, the power of God pouring through the house in waves. Nobody had made it to bed that night!

On arrival at Clifton's Cafeteria the next morning Demos was met by two men. One, who only the previous week had said that the Fellowship was not worth five cents, gave him an envelope. Demos expected it to be a letter of resignation, but he could scarcely believe what he saw—a cheque made payable to the Full Gospel Business Men's Fellowship International for one thousand dollars! This man, Miner Arganbright, had been woken by God early that morning and told that the Fellowship would go round the world and that he was to make the first donation.

Still hardly taking it all in, Demos heard the other man speak to him. He was a printer called Thomas Nickel. While working late at his printing press to catch up on orders the previous night, he heard the Holy Spirit clearly telling him to drive to Los Angeles for that meeting. He lived in Watsonville, 400 miles north of Los Angeles, so he had to drive through the night. He told Demos that he wanted to offer him his press and services. Demos did not understand why Thomas thought he needed a printing press, but he explained that it was to produce a magazine. He, too, had heard the Spirit saying that the Fellowship must go around the world and that therefore it would need a 'voice'. From that meeting onwards, Demos began to see the outworking of the vision that God had given him. Chapters were started all over the United States and in 1956 the word 'International' took on a reality as the first chapter in Canada was opened in Toronto.

2

Destination: London

Over the last twenty years airlifts to different parts of the world have become a regular feature of the FGBMFI, fulfilling the vision of God to be *international*. Before 1965, no one in the Fellowship had envisaged this, but God had prepared the way and the heart of a young Irishman.

Ray Barnett was born in Portstewart, Northern Ireland, in 1936 with few apparent advantages. He was not expected to live but having survived his first few weeks against all the odds, his mother arranged for him to be adopted into a large poverty-stricken family. School days were not happy for Ray, as learning disabilities and slowness of speech made it very difficult for him to communicate.

Leaving school at the age of fourteen he found a job with a photographer in Coleraine. This was the turning point in his life. On his very first morning his employer asked what must have seemed a strange question: 'Do you know if you'll go to heaven when you die, Raymond?' This lay preacher then shared the Gospel with Ray. Later that day, in a simple prayer, Ray asked that he too might be 'born again', and he 'quietly received the unspeakable treasure of eternal life'.

As if to make up for his early disadvantages, God moved rapidly in this young man's life, showing him how much he loved him. A few weeks after committing his life to Jesus Christ, while in a small Sunday morning service, Ray felt a strong urge to stand up and pray. Only once before had he tried to speak in front of a crowd and on that occasion he had fainted. Even now as he stood among that group of Christians, the fear of his halting speech made him feel as if he would faint once again. But God urged him on, and the experience suddenly became very different. A warm burning sensation moved from his throat into his mouth, painless yet fiery, and he found himself speaking—only he did not know what he was saying. The congregation watched and listened in amazement as he spoke fluently and in an unfamiliar foreign language. The group had no Pentecostal tradition and were dumbfounded by this strange happening. Ray knew it was a miracle, for not only had God baptised him in the Holy Spirit but his speech problem was healed from that very moment, never to return.

Following a period of street evangelism, Bible school and pastoral work, God led Ray from Ireland to Canada where he married and began a family. While in Calgary, God directed him into a new career with a well-respected travel agency. His role was to arrange tours for Christian groups and through this he came into contact with the Full Gospel Business Men's Fellowship.

Ray was instrumental in setting up the Calgary chapter of FGBMFI and soon became the Fellowship's youngest International Director. As President of the chapter he invited Jerry Jensen editor of *Voice* Magazine, to be their second speaker. After that breakfast meeting, Ray took Jerry to the world-famous resort of Banff and Lake Louise. As they travelled through the spectacular mountain and forest scenery they spoke about the unique way in which God had led each of them. Later that afternoon, relaxing in the hot springs, Ray told Jerry about his idea of flying two or three jets filled with businessmen into another country, perhaps Britain. Even as he talked about it, Ray's excitement grew. He visualised a convention in London which would reach thousands of people with the Gospel.

Although he was excited by the idea, Jerry was also a little guarded—after all, nothing like this had ever been done before. However, when Ray reassured him that this was his line of business, Jerry decided to ask Demos Shakarian what he thought about the idea. A few days later he phoned Ray: 'You need to get down to Los Angeles on Friday,' he said. 'We've got an appointment with Demos to tell him about your London airlift idea.' As Ray did not have enough money to buy the ticket a financial miracle was needed. But confident in God's ability to provide, he made the booking.

The appointment with Demos had not been easy to arrange. Always busy, he had agreed to see the two men between 11.30 and 11.45 following the Saturday morning breakfast meeting at Clifton's Cafeteria. Ray was concerned that fifteen minutes would not be sufficient to put across such an idea, and he was right. As Demos listened excitedly to the young man talking about his vision, he decided to give over the entire day to discussion of the airlift and by midnight the three men had come to a decision.

An airlift to London was agreed for the 1965 World Convention of FGBMFI. Ray Barnett would be the convention co-ordinator, helped by Jerry Jensen and others. What a challenge for this young Irishman, and what an opportunity! He set out to fire others with enthusiasm for the vision God had given him. In the months following his meeting with Demos in Los Angeles, Ray travelled thousands of miles in the United States and abroad. He aimed to inspire businessmen throughout the world to come to the convention in London and see what God would do there. Meanwhile, God had his men prepared in London.

The 1950s had seen the great crusade at Harringay when Billy Graham and his team, together with many churches, held a three-months' campaign. Even today it is impossible to quantify fully the results of that campaign. Thousands came forward to make a commitment to Jesus Christ, many becoming ministers themselves. The effect was ongoing as church congregations throughout the country began to experience a growing desire for a deeper experience in the Christian life. This was not confined to any specific church or denomination, nor to any particular part of the land. As Andy Milliken writes in *From the Kwai to the Kingdom* 'A vision was beginning to surface for outreach activities, and a new compassion stirred for other Christians wherever they worshipped, and for those who did not know the Lord.'

One example of this stirring was a monthly evening fellowship meal at the YMCA in Tottenham Court Road. About seventy people, mostly businessmen but with some pastors and evangelists, would meet to seek ways of sharing the Gospel using modern techniques. Unfortunately, despite many good ideas, nothing specific came out of these meetings until one night when a pastor from South London stood up and made a suggestion. Was it not time they stopped telling God what they wanted to do and started listening to what God had to say? So simple, yet how many of us still try everything else first before we try God's way?

The outcome was a regular lunchtime prayer meeting in the heart of the city for businessmen working there. This meeting, held in Fleet Street, received a tremendous anointing from the Holy Spirit over the next few years and became known worldwide. Visitors from many countries came and shared with the fellowship. People gave up their lunch in order not to miss what God was doing in that prayer group. Churches of many denominations were encouraged by the experiences of their members who attended the Fleet Street group, particularly as their own prayer meetings grew as a result.

The Fleet Street group received many letters asking about the renewal in Great Britain, particularly from America, and it was from there that an unusual request came in 1965. They were asked if they could arrange a 'steering committee' for a group of Americans who wanted to visit Britain in November. Because of the high-pressure presentations associated with the American Christian scene, the group were cautious, even sceptical. It thus took considerable persuasion before several of them agreed to form such a committee. Although few people in Britain had heard of the FGBMFI, those comprising the steering committee were prepared to step out in faith. These men included the Rev Michael Harper, Andy Milliken, an advertising and public relations consultant, the Rev Ernest Walton-Lewsey, Director of the London Embankment Mission, and William Thompson, a Savile Row tailor who chaired the group. Other men were drawn in to help with the enormous organisation of such a venture.

God had indeed prepared his men in London. William Thompson, or Bill as he became more affectionately known, died in India in 1983. He was a key figure in God's plan for the FGBMFI in Britain. As a Savile Row tailor he visited the United States twice a year to sell his hand-made suits and while there he would take the opportunity to visit churches and religious communities and preach the word of the Lord. His contact with the FGBMFI came about in a remarkable way through Lee Buck. Lee worked for New York Life Insurance Company, supervising more than 10,000 agents and 350 offices in the United States and Canada. He was also a Director of FGBMFI.

In the midst of a very busy day in his Madison Avenue office, Lee received a telephone call from an English gentleman which went something like this:

'Mr Buck, my name is Bill Thompson and I am a friend of Bob Kuenzle. I just thought I would ring you up.'

'Well, Mr Thompson, what can I do for you?'

'Nothing, really. I just wanted to say hello.'

Apart from mentioning the name of his hotel, this was the entire conversation. After a few moments of looking at the work on his desk, Lee began to ponder this rather strange conversation. He couldn't remember anyone called Bob Kuenzle and he had no idea who Bill Thompson might be. The obvious step was to ring his wife, Audrey, and sure enough she reminded him that Bob Kuenzle had spent some time with them while on a business trip in New York. Putting the telephone down, he thought to himself that he had been rather abrupt. If Bill Thompson was a friend of Bob's then he must be a Christian and he had better ring him back quickly. As soon as they were connected he asked, 'Mr Thompson, are you a Christian?'

Through that rather inauspicious beginning came the connection between the Fleet Street group and the FGBMFI, and also a life-long friendship. Bill later met Demos and other members in the United States and in so doing God completed another part of his 'jig-saw puzzle' so that the right men were available at the right time.

Two weeks or so before the airlift, Ray and Jerry flew to London to join the men who were dealing with the final arrangements. It was a mammoth task. Hundreds of hotel reservations had to be made for those coming from America on the three chartered jets. Meeting places had to be booked as well as flights and accommodation for those going on to Europe. In addition, there were hundreds of invitations for teams of individuals to go and speak in churches, colleges, prisons, factories and homes throughout the country. There was such a great demand for speakers and seminars to discuss forming FGBMFI chapters that many of the men involved in organising the teams had hardly slept for days. However, everyone was encouraged by the co-operation of ministers and the friendliness of those contacted for help, including some MPs. As Bill Thompson exclaimed, 'This isn't a convention! This is an appointment with God!'

The realisation of a God-given vision came about on a chilly November morning as the first of the three jets made its final approach and landed at Heathrow. As Ray watched the plane taxi to a halt, he experienced eagerness, mild impatience and a sense of disbelief. So much work had been done in the previous sixteen days. Days which stretched from twelve to eighteen hours. Days in which the telephone had rung almost unceasingly. Days spent rushing to appointments or speaking at meetings. No small wonder that Ray and Jerry felt slightly befuddled, hardly daring to believe that the dream had become a reality.

A sense of relief was also no doubt experienced by the pilot of one of the three planes. While flying over the Atlantic at 33,000 feet, an irregularity was detected. Both pilot and copilot were baffled as there was no visible engineering or hydraulic reason for the fault, so they asked the flight engineer to take a quick look at the rear of the plane. Walking down the long gangway he was taken aback to find no one in any of the passenger seats in the forward section. The reason soon became clear. Entering the rear section he found all the passengers gathered together worshipping God. As politely as possible he ordered them back to their original seats, saying that otherwise they were likely to meet their Maker sooner than envisaged.

On those flights alone, some wonderful testimonies

began to emerge. One man, Miles Smith of Kankakee, Illinois, described himself as eighty years young, but unfortunately he could not prove that he had ever been born. Determined to be part of the airlift, he drove hundreds of miles cross country in wintry weather to find his ninety-year-old brother in order to obtain an affidavit acceptable to the Passport Office. Miles had heard an evangelist say that if you want a blessing from God, you must first make a point of contact. He decided that his would be attending the London convention where he hoped to receive the baptism in the Holy Spirit. At 31,000 feet over the Atlantic, one of the men walked down the aisle of the plane and said, 'Brother Miles, what about praying for you now?' He placed his arms around him and the Lord immediately filled Miles with his Holy Spirit.

Others told how God had met their financial needs by providing unexpected overtime or contracts that had dragged on for months suddenly being completed making finance available. Yet others told how God had healed them and others in miraculous ways. Dr Jere Melilli had booked to go on the trip but just days before departure his medical associate slipped a disc, making it seemingly impossible for him to leave the medical practice in Baton Rouge. However, in answer to prayer the healing power of God touched his associate enabling him to take over the practice so that Dr Jere could go to the convention.

Throughout all three flights, the crew members saw and heard a Christian witness wherever they turned. There was no drinking or smoking, no flirting with the crew, just people praying, singing and praising the Lord. Towards the end of the flight there was a fog warning and it was thought the planes would have to land elsewhere. But as the Christians prayed the fog lifted.

Stepping out of the warm plane into the chilly November morning, Rose Shakarian commented how everything looked so strange and different, as if out of a storybook. Many people must have wondered what had hit London as the enthusiastic Americans took every opportunity to witness for Jesus and tell people why they were there. In the lobby of the Hilton Hotel, on trains and in restaurants, even a 'bobby' on the beat, heard the good news of Jesus Christ. The 1965 World Convention had indeed 'begun to roll'.

3

'This is That'

It was surely no coincidence that on Sunday 14th November *The Sunday Express* carried an article entitled 'The people who "speak" in a language they do not know.' This full-page article had been gathering dust for six months when for no apparent reason *The Sunday Express* dug it out and broke all its own precedents by publishing it just before the arrival of the FGBMFI airlift to London. Asking the question, 'Has one of the mysteries of the early church been revived in our modern age?' the writer, David Sanders, quoted from Acts chapter 2 which graphically describes the day of Pentecost when the Holy Spirit was poured out as promised in Joel 2:28–29.

Unlike the superficial or denigrating articles on Christianity often put out by the media, this particular one gave a thoughtful and open-minded account of a house meeting the writer attended in Oxfordshire where, for the first time, he heard the strange phenomenon of 'speaking in tongues.' Acknowledging the biblical basis for the practice and the growing number of groups experiencing it, he posed and to some extent answered the obvious questions raised. Were the people speaking in tongues speaking in real languages or was it just gibberish? His conclusion was that despite exhaustive inquiries by the Lutheran Church in America, the answer was not clear. He accepted however, that on occasions 'real' languages such as Hebrew, Persian, Arabic and Indian had been recorded.

One of the accusations most frequently levelled by those sceptical of the experience is that individuals make up the tongues as they go along. David Sanders emphatically disagreed with this. 'Try it yourself,' he said. 'See how far you get. You will surprisingly soon run out of ideas for "non-words". The result will be jerky and disjointed. But all tongues speaking has the fluency and form of language, sometimes language of beauty.' He gives two further reasons for rejecting the idea of faking. First, the integrity of those speaking in tongues was beyond question as they were people whose lives of prayer and worship went far deeper than the casual church-goer. Secondly, speaking in tongues was being experienced by widely scattered groups totally unaware of each other's existence.

Another argument, that people who practise speaking in tongues are religious fanatics or on the crackpot fringe, was also firmly squashed. Among the group in Oxfordshire there were people from the scientific and administrative staff at the Harwell Atomic Energy Establishment, some with scientific degrees. In fact, all were very much people of the twentieth century. Against the criticism that speaking in tongues serves no purpose, Sanders quoted those interviewed as testifying to knowing spiritual joy, peace and boldness, an experience akin to that conferred on the disciples on the Day of Pentecost.

Over the three weeks following the publication of this article, many other press writers commented on the phenomenon of speaking in tongues as they reported the events connected with the airlift. The reason for this was the importance placed on this experience by the FGBMFI. As the name of their organisation intimates, they believe in a 'full gospel', one which includes not only salvation but baptism in the Holy Spirit, healing and deliverance. Coverage of their unusual approach by the press was described as 'unprecedented'. The public opened their morning newspapers to read headlines such as: 'Millionaire Demos brings deliverance to the Beatniks of Britain.' 'Big business in Soho.' 'Full Gospel in London.' And in the *Church of England Newspaper*: 'Full Gospel men in Church House.' The stories behind these headlines were equally remarkable.

Among those who had come on the airlift were Jack Brown, Nicky Cruz, Johnny Geminez and others, all of whom had experienced being delivered from drug addiction when they turned their lives over to Jesus Christ. They were the first to be sent out into the Soho area to speak to the beatniks and drug addicts. They did not go to reprimand them for their habit, but to be a living, walking proof of the power of the Holy Spirit to transform seemingly hopeless lives. Describing these reformed dope addicts and delinquents as 'Mr Shakarian's shock troops', Peter Moorhead of *The Sun* reported how some delegates had been despatched as part of a 'Love Jesus' squad before they had even had time to unpack. Even more amazing was that within two days twenty 'youthful derelicts' made a decision to give Jesus a chance to work in their lives. Believing as they do in salvation for the whole man, the FGBMFI brought many of those who committed their lives to the Lord over the following days into the Hilton Hotel.

George Gardner, automobile dealer from New York, hired two rooms in the Hilton and moved all the furniture into one, covering the floor of the other with canvas. Then he hired two barbers who cut the long hair of these newly 'born again' ex-drug addicts. By the time they eventually finished, the floor was covered in hair to a depth of almost six inches. A bath and a new suit of clothes followed, turning them into very smart young people. That was not the end of the story. A very concerned hotel manager rang Demos and told him they would all have to vacate the hotel immediately. Demos could not get any sense out of him so a group of men went down to talk with him. The manager was quite distraught but adamant that they should leave. He accused them of bringing large numbers of beatniks into his hotel and then hiding them in their rooms. They took him up to the room where the 'clean-up' operation was taking place and he could not believe his eyes. Needless to say, he then relented and allowed everyone to stay.

An account by John Sherrill entitled 'London's Strange Society' gives the story of a typical Soho drug addict. Harry, a school drop-out with no future in his job, had left Belfast and hitch-hiked to London. Drifting around the city trying to get casual work and with nowhere to go, he was met one night by a young man in blue jeans, an oversize suit coat, hair down to his shoulders, and sporting an earring. This young man did what John Sherrill says Christians should have been doing, he met Harry's need by inviting him to become part of his group—young people who were also lonely and without homes or jobs. They shared what they had with him in the way of food, places to sleep, and, of course, dope and alcohol. Fortunately for Harry and those like him, a young preacher named Vic Ramsey had just started to work among the beatniks of Soho, taking with him the promise of a Lord who could heal disease, take away sorrows and loneliness, and bring about a complete change in a person's life. Vic had opened a basement in Orange Street Congregational Church just off Leicester Square and it was to this place that the 'shock troops' were sent.

One member of the team began to keep a list of all the beatniks who had been converted. But eventually there were so many that he lost track. However, he did record some wonderful stories not only of these young people receiving the full gospel for themselves but of returning with their friends that they too might share the same experience. John was one such young man. One night he brought his room-mate, Freddy, to meet the men who had befriended him. Freddy was a very young looking twenty-four-year old who came from a well-to-do background. He had run away from home and had been using dope for six years. At Westminster Chapel that night he was saved and baptised in the Holy Spirit. Through his witness, he in turn won many others to the Lord.

Gene was thirty-nine but unlike Freddy he looked at least fifty or more. He had been next in line for the English fly-weight boxing championship when he became hooked on drugs and had to give up his sport. For many years Gene had been controlled by his addiction, but that week in the Metropolitan Tabernacle he too came to know Jesus and was baptised in the Holy Spirit.

Johnny was typical of many young people in Soho. Having got himself into trouble once in his home town of Newcastle, he discovered that people expected trouble from him all the time. He had been involved in theft and was sent to a correctional institute but found it impossible to fit back into school where he was constantly under suspicion. Like many others he ended up hanging around London's 'square mile of evil', an angry young man. Johnny saw his former associates accept Jesus and undergo not only a spiritual transformation but also a physical one. He eventually decided to try the former, but he was determined to hang on to his long hair—it was his badge of disdain for society. Although he had decided to give his life to Christ, deep within his anger and bitterness were tearing him apart. A few days later he received the baptism of the Holy Spirit and was free to forgive. The next day, with only a fraction of hesitation he allowed the barber to cut the first huge handful of hair. Later he reappeared clean and shining, ready for a new start in life.

Marilyn Crudo from Los Angeles described her reaction during the first meeting in the Orange Street basement. As she looked around her at the young people with long hair and strange clothes she recalls:

'I looked at my nice clothes, ran my fingers through my clean hair and felt ashamed! I never knew anything like this existed. I had to come clear across the ocean, down into the basement of an old church in London, to find out just how wonderful it is to be a Christian!'

That night she met a young fifteen-year-old girl known as 'Tiger'. Small, helpless and unloved, when told she was loved she looked with blurred and bloodshot eyes and said, 'I don't want to be loved, and I love no one.' Walking into the meeting in the Hilton Hotel the following evening, Marilyn saw Tiger and was thrilled when she gave her heart to the Lord and said with a beaming smile, 'God loves me!' Having been filled with the Holy Spirit and spoken in new tongues, she at last knew the true meaning of freedom and was able to throw away her drugs.

This aspect of the airlift's work inevitably caught the imagination of the press more than any other. They followed the teams wherever they went, photographing and interviewing the new converts. There was, of course, a great deal of scepticism and Demos Shakarian was asked how genuine he believed the conversions were. 'Of course, we can be fooled,' he said, 'even taken for a ride by some of the people we help. We expect that. Others attempt to change their lives but slip back into their old ways despite our help. But if only one person here starts a completely new life—and in doing so shows an example to many others—well, then every cent of what we spend here and every minute of our time in Britain will have been worth it.' As the press pointed out, the convention in hotel and air fares alone was costing about £85,000—all to be met out of the delegates' pockets. But one fact was very difficult to explain away. The ex-drug addicts showed their arms to the reporters who saw that the needle marks had miraculously healed and they were completely free of any withdrawal symptoms.

Reporters, Granada television, BBC radio, local policemen and even Scotland Yard descended on the Hilton Hotel and Soho to see what was going on. They were astounded to hear that one man had donated enough money to send several young men on the trip, all former drug addicts but healed and filled with the Holy Spirit. Among those who went out into Soho with the team was a narcotics officer from Scotland Yard. Like many doctors and others who worked with addicts, he believed that it was impossible for anyone hooked on drugs ever to be totally freed from the habit. In amazement he watched as addicts responded to the call to give their life to Jesus Christ and were immediately baptised in the Holy Spirit and spoke in tongues. He saw their lives transformed as they stopped using drugs without any withdrawal symptoms and returned to work. Not surprisingly, he was one of three London policemen who also became Christians that week.

But it was not all Soho and beatniks. The convention had been advertised as: 'From North America to Great Britain . . . in the power of the Holy Spirit . . . Phase one—LONDON—a convention for revival'. Although the first public meeting was on Wednesday evening in Westminster Chapel, the day started with a seven o'clock prayer meeting followed by a breakfast meeting at eight o'clock, and after-service sessions of prayer with those wanting salvation or baptism in the Holy Spirit. The opening session was a little stiff at first as the Americans and British felt strange with each other, but when they began to sing the Spirit of the Lord began to move. It was a truly international and interdenominational gathering and one minister was moved to exclaim, 'For twenty years I have been a pastor, but never have I experienced a crusade where there was such a spirit of unity as prevailed in the spiritual airlift to London.' Derek Prince shared his testimony and gave a ringing call for Christian laymen as well as clergy to join in the latter-day revival. The prayer rooms were full and most of the people there had never seen so many baptised in the Spirit in such a short time.

One of the most amazing aspects of the convention was the number of people who went to London not knowing what it was about but feeling impelled by God to be there. Many had never experienced breakfast and luncheon meetings in a hotel, and some thought that perhaps the Hilton Hotel was too luxurious. God showed one man quite clearly why the convention wasn't based at an inexpensive small hotel. As he went up to his room on one occasion, an African gentleman in a multi-coloured, richly embroidered robe and turban swept into the lift and returned his greeting with dignity. On being invited to attend the revival meeting at the Royal Albert Hall that night, the dignitary very promptly and graciously accepted. As he left the lift one of the other men gasped, 'Do you know who that is? That's the Vice Premier of Nigeria!' They had to be in the Hilton Hotel to meet the people God wanted to touch.

On the last day of the convention two meetings were held in the Royal Albert Hall. In the afternoon Nicky Cruz addressed over 7,000 young people, and Oral Roberts was the guest speaker at the final evening meeting. If ever there was a doubt that the Christians of this country were open to knowing more of the power of the Holy Spirit, the World Convention and especially the Saturday evening in the Royal Albert Hall dispelled any such claim. The Hall, which holds around 5,000 people, was packed to capacity with many thousands more left outside unable to get in.

Some twenty or so years later, those who attended that evening still vividly remember it. It was not the singing or the preaching, or even the countless people who responded to the final appeal that made such a deep impression. At the end of his inspiring address Oral Roberts asked everyone to stand and speak out loud in tongues. Although many people in Britain had experienced baptism in the Holy Spirit, they had never spoken out loud in tongues in a public meeting in such a way. The effect was electrifying. One long-time pentecostal minister described it as a manifestation of God's power which made history. He had never known it happen anywhere before. It was this perhaps, more than anything else, that characterised the FGBMFI among other interdenominational organisations. It experienced 'that which was spoken of by the prophet Joel: "And it shall come to pass in the last days," saith God, "I will pour of my Spirit upon all flesh; and your sons and your daughters shall prophesy, and your young men shall see visions, and your old men shall dream dreams; and on my servants and on my handmaidens I will pour out in those days of my Spirit", . . .'

The convention may have ended that Saturday night but it was only a small part of the work accomplished. Meetings for church leaders formed a very important part of the programme. Three seminars were held, two luncheon ones in the Hilton Hotel for ministers and students, and then on the Monday following the convention yet another in Westminster Church House. Over eleven hundred people attended altogether, much of the success being due to Michael Harper who worked tirelessly in and for the seminars. At the latter meeting the theme was charismatic renewal. About six hundred ministers and special guests came and over twenty-five ministers received the baptism in the Holy Spirit. In seminars held by the various teams around the country some thirty ministers were also filled with the Holy Spirit.

During the second week of the trip, delegates were divided into teams and travelled all over Britain as well as many European countries. It would take a book in itself to describe all the marvellous things that happened, so perhaps just a few stories will give the flavour.

One group in Newcastle witnessed to approximately three thousand, either in group meetings or by personal ministry. They saw fifty people commit their lives to Jesus Christ, twenty-two baptised in the Holy Spirit and four miraculously healed. Two people testified to having received the Holy Spirit after reading *VOICE Magazine*, one a minister of a mission and the other a Baptist minister.

Judge Kermit Bradford had breakfast with some fifteen barristers at the Ivanhoe Hotel. The group was led by a Queen's Counsellor, Mr Poson. At the other end of the scale a doctor from New Mexico witnessed to a young boy of fifteen in a Wimpy bar and he accepted Jesus as his personal saviour. That alone would have made the doctor's trip worth while, but two days later he met the young man, Raymond, to give him a New Testament. At the Wimpy bar he found Raymond witnessing to another young man about Jesus. As he saw the doctor approaching he said, 'Here he comes now. He will finish telling you about Jesus.'

Another team went to Christ College, Cambridge, where the students listened intently to the various testimonies. On subsequent evenings, three students gave their lives to Jesus Christ and eight were baptised in the Holy Spirit. One group visited a pastor and his wife in Darlington and were able to speak to the students in the teacher training college. This pastor later wrote about the tremendous effect of the visit, not only on the students but also on their own small church. They had decided to launch a literature crusade involving the college and 100,000 homes which would receive a special leaflet. This explained what it really meant to trust in Christ and laid special emphasis upon baptism in the Holy Spirit. Such a venture was a tremendous step of faith for such a small group, but they felt they must follow up what had been begun by the team's visit.

Wales, Scotland, the Isle of Wight, Guernsey, Sweden, Ireland, Italy, Sicily, Holland, France and Spain were visited by members of the airlift. The contingent to France had a unique opportunity to visit a gypsy camp near Paris where there were a number of Christians. They spoke a variety of languages including Romany. One member of the team spoke Spanish which was then interpreted into French and then English. Despite the language difficulties, they felt the Spirit of God in a most marvellous way in that packed church. Many came forward for healing and one for salvation.

In Rome the team were handing out leaflets for the service. One high-ranking communist official angrily stamped his into the ground. However, the young people of the church persuaded him to attend a meeting. Although he sat right at the back, he could not evade the power of God. That night he went forward to give his life to Jesus. He returned the following evening with two former comrades who were also saved. Not content, on the third evening he brought his wife, son and daughter-in-law, all of whom gave their hearts to Jesus Christ. Almost everyone who went forward for salvation in those meetings also received the fullness of the Holy Spirit.

When the teams were being decided for the second week of this World Convention, one lieutenant colonel in the United States Airforce, being of Swedish and Danish descent, longed to join a team going to either country. But his 'military orders' were for England only. However, he met a Swedish Christian who asked him to go to Sweden. He decided that the only thing to do was to put it into the Lord's hands, and in less than half an hour, through an unknown embassy contact, he had his clearance for Sweden. After speaking to hundreds of young people at a rally sponsored by the Swedish FGBMFI, the Lord confirmed his word as many came forward for salvation and baptism in the Holy Spirit.

Back in England, Pat Robertson was thrilled to have the opportunity of making two BBC radio broadcasts. The final meeting of the convention in the Metropolitan Tabernacle was also broadcast. This was an exciting night. Teams had returned from all over Britain and Europe to share what God had been doing, and many of those who had come to know the Lord or been blessed through their ministry also came to be part of the farewell service. Some of the young people from Soho shared how the Lord had touched them as well as a prisoner who had served thirty-one years but had come to know the Lord during the convention.

Ray Barnett's vision of plane-loads of men flying out to another country to share the Gospel had more than come to pass. But another vision was also becoming a reality—the vision that God had given Demos nearly thirteen years before of how he was going to bring men all over the world back to spiritual life and vitality.

4

Appointment with God

There are times in many people's lives when they know without any shadow of doubt that God has put them in a particular place for a particular purpose. So it was for Bill Thompson when he declared in the Albert Hall, 'This is an appointment with God.'

Bill had made himself completely available to God and he was thrilled when Ray Barnett, whom he had met in the States, rang to ask him to take the chairmanship of the steering committee. Before the Second World War, Bill and his wife, Betty, had been members of the London Crusade Choir under the leadership of Douglas Gray and every Easter they held a meeting at the Royal Albert Hall. When Bill phoned Douglas to ask how he went about organising it, Douglas naturally asked what was going to happen and who the speakers would be. Bill rattled off a few names such as Harold Bredesen and Derek Prince only to be asked, 'Who are they? Nobody knows them.' When Bill explained that it didn't matter who the speakers were Douglas was somewhat taken aback. So he asked if they had a choir or a soloist but the answer was no on both counts. His advice to Bill was to forget the whole thing. There was no way they could do it unless they had a big name to attract people.

Undaunted, Bill went to see the manager of the Albert Hall, had a long talk with him and made the booking. The committee then organised publicity. Within a short time the manager rang Bill and told him there was no need to worry because, from many years' experience he knew by the response to the publicity that the place would be filled.

No wonder Bill's faith had been inspired on that wonderful last day of the convention when God moved in such miraculous ways to bring salvation, healing and the infilling of the Holy Spirit to those in the Albert Hall. It was estimated by ministers involved that two thousand people had been baptised in the Holy Spirit at that evening meeting. Sharing about this experience some fourteen years later in Ireland, Bill talked of the number of people 'just passing through' London that day who found themselves in that gathering. One man had been involved with a group of missionaries in the Far East who had been filled with the Holy Spirit. He just walked into the convention where God also baptised him with the Spirit. Many years later he sought Bill out to share what the Lord had done for him.

Bill was inspired not only to start a London chapter of the FGBMFI, but also to set up a Christian centre for some of the drug addicts who had come to know the Lord during the convention. Many of the Americans who had much experience in this work were concerned that the young men especially were taken out of the London drug scene and given an opportunity to become established in the Christian faith. They encouraged Bill to look for a suitable place and when he saw an advertisement for Turnours Hall he took the first possible train to go and view the property. As he was travelling he lifted up his right arm and asked the Lord not to allow him to sign anything if it was not in his will. As it happened, he felt it right to buy the house, costing the then staggering sum of £20,000, and returned to London to tell Demos and the others before they returned to the States.

At that time Bill had no plans to run the home himself, particularly as he had a minister and his wife staying with him who were anxious to work in that sphere. Much to his surprise and dismay, they turned down the opportunity. So, true to character and with no fuss, Bill and his wife packed up their belongings and moved into Turnours Hall. Eventually it became a conference centre rather than a Christian hostel and many have spoken of the blessings they have received there.

The London chapter of the FGBMFI began to meet regularly at the Bonnington Hotel and it was in one of those meetings that the Lord spoke to a young student. His name was Roger Price. At the 1983 Blackpool Convention of the Fellowship, Roger shared what was both an amusing but at the same time an awesome experience. Roger had been an atheist before coming to know the Lord in 1966. He now wanted everything God had. One night in 1967 he hitch-hiked his way to the Bonnington Hotel as he had heard about the meetings where people received the baptism in the Holy Spirit. Although he had a great desire for God, he was still a young Christian and very sceptical, so he was amazed to find that he had to pay to get in. The cost was £1 which seemed very steep to a student on a grant of between £60 and £66 for a whole year. Wondering what on earth he was going to do, and not realising that a Christian could pray about such matters, he devised what he thought was an ingenious scheme. He stood outside the hotel looking just as he thought a non-Christian should look. As these people were keen to lead others to Christ, it seemed a good way to get in. He leaned against the wall, supposedly chewing gum, and within two minutes a lady came up and said, 'Excuse me, but there is a Christian meeting going on, would you like to come in?' Trying not to seem too positive, Roger agreed and she paid for him to get in. After that introduction, someone was always willing to pay for him.

During the meetings, Roger always sat at the back. At the third meeting someone at the front gave a prophecy in which God said that there were five people in the gathering he wanted to use and that he had special ministries for them. Still sceptical, Roger wondered how many there really were. But then Bill Thompson confirmed that this was a word from the Lord and he felt that five people should come down to the front and be prayed for. After that he prayed that the Lord would first prevent these people from moving and then catapult them out of their seats to the front. As Roger was somewhat cynically thinking that they would probably get about fourteen, he suddenly felt as if a fire had been lit under his seat. 'I am not going out,' he kept repeating to himself, 'this is ridiculous. They are asking for five ad if I go down there I'll be the sixth and then there'll be a big inquest as to who is out of the Spirit.' Just as he had determined he would not move he found himself running out to the front—and to his amazement he was the fifth.

The men at the front, all 'big' names whom Roger did not even dare say hello to in those days, came down to pray for them. They started at the other end from Roger and gathered around the first man. As they laid hands on him the word was that he would be an evangelist and thousands would be converted through him. The next person would be a healer and the next was to have a ministry of deliverance. By this time, Roger was getting very concerned that they wouldn't be able to think of anything by the time they got to him. After praying for the fourth man they finally came to Roger. There was a long ominous silence and Roger wished he had never come down to the front. Then one of the men began to cry and to sob. Roger remembered how 'there was a sobbing mass of humanity around me. It went on so long I wanted to say, "I know I'm bad, but not as bad as all that!" '

It was then that the word of the Lord came and it was simply this: 'My son, you will be known for your love of me and men will be inspired by your love for me.'

Roger emphasised how grateful he was for the men in the FGBMFI who were open to the Holy Spirit in those days. As many will know, God used Roger in a mighty way to bring his word to the body of Christ all over the world. Even after his death in 1987, his ministry continues, through tapes, to be a tremendous blessing.

There were, of course, many others who came into contact with God in a new and dynamic way through the meetings at the Bonnington Hotel. Two women, one Brethren and the other Anglo-Catholic, were invited to a dinner where they received the baptism in the Holy Spirit. One of them, Madge Fraser, was already in her sixties when the Lord led her to take Bibles into Hungary. She made sixteen of these trips before being severely interrogated and forbidden ever to return. The story of this woman's remarkable experiences can be read in *Unfinished Journey* (New Wine Press).

In those early days following the airlift, chapters were also set up in Preston, Belfast, Birmingham and Southampton. In view of the initial impact of the airlift, this was perhaps a very small number, and not all of them even survived. But they kept alive the vision God had given of men reaching out to other men and coming together to worship and praise God.

Preston was the first chapter to be set up in England and still remains vibrant to the present day. Their first President, Aubrey Birchall, had been in the South of England where he met a Pentecostal believer, Reg

Down who, like Bill Thompson, was a tailor. Reg mentioned the forthcoming airlift from the States, saying that in addition to the London Convention, groups would be sent out all over the country. He asked if Aubrey would be willing to organise some meetings in Lancashire. At that time Aubrey was the Health Education Officer for Preston and his job was sufficiently flexible to allow him to take time for this work.

On his return to Preston he sent letters to scores of ministers and laymen whom he thought might be interested in an FGBMFI chapter. Only twenty-four came to the first meeting. All but two were from the historic Pentecostal churches and there was not a lot of encouragement for the idea. However, Aubrey was so convinced that God wanted it to happen that he determined to forge ahead regardless. In due course, Reg Down telephoned to ask how many delegates he should send to Preston and in sheer faith Aubrey asked for eighteen. A team of sixteen men and women arrived on the 28th November 1965 led by Enoch Christoffersen, then considered to be the largest independent turkey processor in the United States. Later that week Robert Carrington, the pastor from Enoch's home town arrived to lead meetings at Lancaster University. The other team members shared their testimonies in churches and schools in Preston, Wigan, Bolton and Blackburn, their witness characterised by a contagious enthusiasm for the Lord.

On the last day of that memorable week, a united meeting was held in the Co-operative Assembly Hall when Aubrey's own ten-year-old daughter, Sharon, was baptised in the Holy Spirit along with others. Sharon was the first person that Art Nersasian, a member of the team and nephew of Demos, had ever prayed for to receive this experience. It was an exciting night and at the close Enoch Christoffersen gathered a group of men together and suggested the formation of a chapter. With

Aubrey as President, David Spurdle, Secretary, and John Spence and Bernard Myerscough making up the officers, the chapter held its first dinner meeting in Booth's Café in December 1965. Thirty-three men joined to form the chapter which later received its Charter (official recognition of joining the Fellowship) from Bill Thompson.

In January 1987 a special anniversary dinner was held to celebrate its twenty-one years of spreading the good news. The local newspaper included an article entitled 'Chapter 21' and commented that it was the first group of its kind in this country, although now there were some 280 chapters 'and the groups are constantly growing'. On that evening, three former presidents of the chapter, including Aubrey Birchall, were present from as far afield as the States and Australia.

Information about the early groups is not easy to find, but Ted Kent, now living in South Africa, recalls those early days with great affection. Ted had heard of the airlift and booked himself into the Hilton Hotel for the week of the convention. He and some friends arrived in the hotel foyer shortly after Demos Shakarian and others from the States. He remembers how the whole atmosphere of the foyer was charged with the power of God. Not knowing who they were, Demos walked across to introduce himself and immediately began to prophesy over one member of the group, every single word of which has since come to pass. Ted attended both the Southampton and London chapters, as well as visiting Birmingham from time to time, and was thrilled to see many lives touched by God.

One of the features of those involved in the early chapters, which was evidenced again in the late 1970s and 80s, was the way they travelled to support each other. Bill Thompson would leave straight after work to drive up to Birmingham for their Friday evening dinner meeting and those in Birmingham would set off at the crack of dawn to go to a breakfast meeting either in London or Preston. There was a tremendous sense of excitement and wonder at the way God was moving in the Fellowship. Men were prepared to make physical and financial sacrifices, almost afraid to miss out on what was taking place. Of course, the charismatic movement had not yet begun to move across this country and for many Christians the FGBMFI seemed somewhat extreme in its enthusiasm and belief that it was simply continuing what had begun in the Book of Acts and had been experienced by many groups throughout the history of the Christian church.

The formation of the Birmingham chapter came about through a man called Walter Day. During the Second World War he had been stationed in Preston where they held a 'Forces Rally' every Sunday evening. Walter led the meetings with the help of a pianist and a song-leader called Sam Thompson whose brother Bill would come up occasionally to speak for them. When Bill became involved with organising the airlift, he contacted Walter who by then had moved to Castle Bromwich. Like so many others, Walter was tremendously blessed and encouraged by the London convention and by subsequent visits to Turnours Hall. He felt a need to set up a chapter in Birmingham but at that time he didn't know of anyone else who could help. Nothing daunted, he decided to go it alone with Bill Thompson and Ted Kent, travelling to Birmingham each month until it became established.

'At that time,' says Walter, 'people were wary of spending money on a meal, so we just had coffee and biscuits.' Nevertheless, quite a good number would come, often as many as seventy. Walter Wainwright, who had been in contact with FGBMFI in the United States and Canada, and Les Ashwood joined with Walter Day and together they ran the Birmingham chapter for about seven years. During that time they were greatly encouraged by the Fountain Trust, set up by the Rev Michael Harper who came to Birmingham and would sometimes speak at the chapter. This was not structured as most groups are today, and they rarely booked speakers, preferring to leave it open to the leading of the Holy Spirit, but they saw God move in wonderful ways. They recall one evening when the speaker, a missionary, hobbled into the meeting with a severely strained ankle. In the worship time they began to sing the chorus 'Walk in the light'. As they were singing, the missionary felt a touch from God and walked to the front of the meeting. She told everyone that she believed the Lord had healed her ankle and to demonstrate the fact she took off the bandage and proceeded to dance and worship the Lord.

A number of people from Coventry came to the meetings of the Birmingham group, so after some time a chapter was set up there. Coventry Cathedral gave them the use of the lecture hall of its unusual new building free of charge. At the first meeting, as in Birmingham, they just had coffee and biscuits. About seventy people came to this meeting where the speakers were two sisters from the Evangelical Sisters of Mary in Darmstadt, West Germany. They had a unique way of worshipping the Lord in singing and dance which delighted everyone. The two Walters leading the meeting, having a similar sense of humour, were rather amused as they sang 'He is high and lifted up, and His train fills the temple'. Underneath the lecture room ran a railway line and the train chose that particular moment to go roaring by below them.

For many people the FGBMFI has been the means of opening up new ministries. From the late 1960s until 1972, Walter Day, Ted Kent, Bill Thompson and one or two others regularly went behind the Iron Curtain to visit persecuted Christians. As a result of this Walter

Day was asked to go to the Soviet Union on behalf of Christian Mission to the Communist World founded by Richard Wurmbrand. Eventually he moved to Canada and travelled extensively as a representative of that organisation, speaking in churches, schools, colleges and home groups as well as mainline radio and television stations. He continues to minister for FGBMFI and is a member of the London, Ontario, chapter. Walter Wainwright also emigrated to the United States, where he died very suddenly in January 1988.

Before looking at the beginning of the FGBMFI in Ireland and the tremendous way in which God has moved in that land, this may be the point at which to ask a difficult question. Why is it, after the tremendous impact of the airlift, the number of teams sent out, and the apparent enthusiasm for the aims of the Fellowship, that so few chapters were established and of these only Preston and Belfast have stayed the course? Much thought and discussion has been given to this and the concensus seems to suggest that the major reason was the lack of Spirit-filled people in this country. Not until the charismatic movement had really taken hold did the FGBMFI see the kind of growth one might have expected in those early days. The Birmingham and Coventry chapters closed in the 1970s because there were not enough men able and willing to take over the leadership when Walter Day and Walter Wainwright left.

In addition to the problem of insufficient men for leadership, the Fellowship was not well organised in this country. Bill Thompson had been encouraged by the American FGBMFI men to open Turnours Hall and I believe his involvement in this project sidetracked him from developing the work of the Fellowship at this time. Lack of communication between the groups in Britain and also between them and the States appears to have been another factor in the early difficulties of the Fellowship.

Walter Wainwright has drawn the analogy with the death and resurrection of Jesus. The greatest works came not before, but after these events, and FGBMFI was on the verge of becoming extinct in the United Kingdom when God stepped in and breathed new life into it.

5

Across the Divide—The Same Kind of Love

One of the most beautiful things about the FGBMFI is the way in which the denominational barriers of the Christian church are put to one side. Men and women come together on the grounds of knowing and acknowledging Jesus Christ as their Lord and Saviour, and believing in the infilling of the Holy Spirit. Nowhere is this better displayed than in the strife-torn country of Ireland where Catholics and Protestants work together as one to bring men and women to know Jesus Christ.

While Preston may rightly be proud of being the first chapter in England, Ireland claims the first in the United Kingdom. Little is known about it in terms of its impact or life-span and in fact very few people in this country knew of its existence. The information came to light in the September 1957 edition of *Full Gospel Men's Voice* (the forerunner of the present *Voice Magazine*). This was a special convention issue to celebrate the 1957 Chicago Convention at which men such as William Branham, David du Plessis, Lester Sumrall and Tommy Hicks were among the well-known speakers.

On 7th July 1957 an eagerly awaited moment arrived. Thomas Nickel, Miner Arganbright and Paul Cain flew in to Belfast from Chicago. As soon as they stepped off the plane they felt that God had arranged the visit and was with them in a special way. They had a brief tour of Southern Ireland, visiting Dublin, Cork, Killarney and Limerick with a view to arranging a campaign and possibly some chapters at a future date. Their main event, however, was a three-day Gospel and Divine Healing Campaign at Wellington Hall, Belfast.

The first evening saw the hall packed to capacity and many people were unable to come in. Both the following evenings saw crowds of a similar size, and over the three days many people came to know Jesus as Saviour and hundreds came for healing. Prayer requests came from all over the country as well as England, Scotland and Wales, and 'miracles were done in the mighty name of Jesus'.

An important outcome of this visit occurred on the last afternoon when quite a number of businessmen gathered with a view to forming an FGBMFI chapter in Belfast. Robert Robinson, who had visited the FGBMFI convention in Minneapolis some two years previously, spoke of what he saw the Fellowship was doing and the blessing it was to everyone. Having a chapter in Belfast, he believed, would help to unite God's people and enable them to rise above narrow-mindedness and denominationalism. He thanked God for the fellowship and sense of oneness experienced during the campaign and trusted that this would be a feature of the chapter in the coming days. 'All can be one in working for the salvation of souls and the healing of bodies.'

Thomas Nickel, from the United States, gave a final word on what the Fellowship was accomplishing throughout the States and in other parts of the world. He told how people from different denominations had come to breakfasts and conventions (sometimes out of curiosity) and had received the baptism in the Holy Spirit, going back into their own churches and fellowships to tell them what God had done. After everyone had spoken, it was decided to establish a chapter in Belfast with Robert Robinson as President, James Johnston Vice President, DC McQuilken as Secretary, and J Somerville as Treasurer.

It was fully expected that the Belfast chapter would be instrumental in opening others in cities such as Dublin and Cork where a tremendous interest had been shown, but this did not come to fruition. Nothing more is known about the group but it was probably due to them that American *Voice Magazine* continued to come to Ireland, paving the way for a tremendous move of God in the coming years.

Billy Burke was one of those who regularly received the American *Voice Magazine*, passed on to him by his father-in-law. In 1965 he saw the advertisement for the world convention in London and knew with absolute certainty that he had to go. This was the Sunday prior to the convention beginning on the Wednesday so he rang his cousin, George Allen, a big businessman, to see if he was interested in going. Billy was a Presbyterian elder and George was the co-ordinator for all Protestant faiths of Northern Ireland, a strong conservative evangelical. Interested but cautious, George decided to ask another friend, Bobby Busby, to go with them and so the three arrived at the Hilton Hotel in November 1965.

After booking in at the Hilton they went down to the luncheon meeting. Billy can recall looking round and knowing he was where he should be, right in the presence of God. Sitting at their table was an American couple from Oklahoma, Cleason and Morine McNutt. In the Hilton, to foreign eyes, they were classed as wealthy Americans but they were actually very far from that. They were 'raw bone' folk from farming stock and had had to borrow the money to come to London. They had seen God work in miraculous ways and shared these experiences with the three men from Northern Ireland. As a result, Billy was baptised in the Holy Spirit and at the end of the convention he went back to Ireland determined to start a chapter of the Fellowship in Belfast. His resolve was strengthened by a prophetic word given to them by Oral Roberts that there would be a work of the Fellowship in their country.

George Allen invited the McNutts to come and minister in Ireland during the week following the convention. He wanted them to speak at a number of meetings to introduce the baptism of the Holy Spirit which was only familiar in the Pentecostal churches. They had many opportunities to witness and testify of the baptism in the Holy Spirit, including at a livestock auction in front of hundreds of Irish farmers. At weekends, the planes from Belfast to London were crowded and the McNutts had reservations for the 10 am flight on Friday morning. That morning Billy Burke rang to say that a man from the Presbyterian church, where they had witnessed, wanted them to pray for him to receive the baptism. They told him that they had a flight to catch for London in order to return to the United States, but he replied that God had plenty of planes and he would get reservations on the plane two hours later. Although the airline had told Cleason that all seats on that flight were booked, Billy was full of faith and phoned the airport. Two people had just cancelled their seats on the later flight so there was no problem! They hurried to the home of the man seeking prayer and, with God so obviously in the business, he was soon filled with the Holy Spirit. They arrived at the airport just five minutes before flight time.

To the people of Ireland the McNutts were unique. Some of the Pentecostal evangelists had created a lot of problems in Ireland because they had emphasised the financial aspects of their ministry. They were remarkable people of faith. Having booked their flight home, no-one was aware that they did not have the money to pay for it. Nevertheless, they walked up to the desk and just as the girl was punching the information into the machine, one of the Irish men just slipped his credit card across the counter, saying, 'They are our guests.'

The McNutts were not the only visitors to Ireland. A report put out by FGBMFI Headquarters records the experience of Mr and Mrs James Johnston. Unfortunately, it has not been possible to discover whether it was the same James Johnston who had been made Vice-President of that first chapter in Belfast and who had later emigrated to the United States. The account talks about the privilege they felt in witnessing in the church which his wife attended as a girl, so it could well be one and the same person. Their experience was quite remarkable.

Having arrived in Belfast, they were walking down a street quite late at night when a man walked up and simply said he had come to meet them. They had made no prior arrangements and as far as they were aware no one knew they were going. However, God had spoken to this man, Pastor Edgar of the Assembly of God Church. He then told them he was interested in getting a chapter of the FGBMFI started. They, too, ministered in a number of places all over Ireland and saw God move in mighty ways.

Trying to piece together the story of the FGBMFI in Ireland is like trying to complete a jig-saw. It seems as if God was working in so many different peoples' lives and then suddenly they all came together. Hector Crory from Newcastle had also been receiving issues of the American *Voice Magazine* without knowing where they came from. Like Billy Burke and others, he was excited by what he read. The testimonies were of ordinary fellows just like him and he wanted to see God moving in Ireland as he was in America.

Shortly after coming back from the London convention, Billy Burke's wife persuaded him that they should go to Newcastle on holiday. He was very reluctant but she insisted. At that stage he was not sure how to go about organising a chapter, so he asked his wife what he should do. On that particular morning she told him to go and walk in some hills not far away and pray that the Lord would give him direction. Later that day they were walking along the promenade when they were stopped by a man, who said, 'You were at the convention in London, I believe?' It was Hector Crory. He told Billy of his desire to see a chapter in Belfast and asked if he would be prepared to join. God had answered Billy's prayer and brought together, in a remarkable way, the men who were to lead this work.

The Lord had his hand on another man in Northern Ireland called Jim Fleming. He had been given a copy of *Voice Magazine* by a leader in their Holiness Presbyterian Church. A bundle of these magazines had appeared in the church but no one knew where they had come from. This particular issue featured the London convention. The remarkable thing was that Jim had seen the 1957 *Voice Magazine* which told of that first chapter in Ireland and as he read through it suddenly dawned on him that this was the same thing! Jim had great difficulty in accepting some of the happenings, particularly as he was suspicious of anything American, especially pentecostal. However, he went along to a couple of dinners in Belfast. Shortly afterwards he was in church one Sunday night when a man leaned over and simply said, 'You come from Ballymena. Arrange a meeting for FGBMFI and we will come.'

In considering the growth of the Fellowship in Ireland we need to understand the background and character of the men who began the work in the 1960s. They were all from very traditional evangelical backgrounds and, with the exception of Hector Crory, rather suspicious of anything pentecostal. George Allen, as co-ordinator for all Protestant faiths in Northern Ireland, was a well-respected member of the Christian community, a solid and reliable Christian.

Jim Fleming came from a Christian background but his father had died when he was only three weeks old. He knew what it was to experience hardship as his mother had struggled to bring him up. As a young man, trying to make sense of an unequal world, he was drawn to the writings of Karl Marx and saw in communism the way forward to a classless and just society. But God stepped in and brought him to a knowledge of Jesus Christ as Saviour and Lord and from that moment on he has never wavered in his belief that Jesus is the only way. Jim is a man of strong character and deep convictions, not easily swayed by others.

Hector Crory, again from a Christian home, was so angered by his parents' conversion, particularly when they became Pentecostals, that he left home at the age of eighteen and without informing his parents signed up for the British Army. So deep was his resentment that when they traced him and came to the barracks to see him, he refused to go outside and meet them. Although his parents were not 'Orange' people, the rest of the family were, and he always considered himself to be an 'Orangeman'. Equal to Hector's hatred for evangelical Christianity was his intense hatred for Roman Catholics.

It was not until many years later, when he had seven beautiful sons (two sets of twins), that he gave any thought to God. He knew he had a responsibility for his children's spiritual state, so he decided to start taking them to church. One weekend he went, much against his inclination, to a meeting at a Baptist church. As he walked in he was full of criticism of everything he saw and heard, but during the last hymn God broke through to him and he began to weep. That night he gave his heart to the Lord. Soon afterwards he was baptised in the Holy Spirit and it was then for the first time in his life that he was able to love Roman Catholics. God was preparing him, and the others, for a special work.

The Belfast chapter had a tremendous impact. In its early days three to four hundred people would come along, and even in the troubles of the 1970s people still continued to come, though in far less numbers. By that time they were meeting in the Europa Hotel, the most bombed of hotels, and they were the only organisation that continued to meet regularly in that place throughout those difficult years. The Ballymena chapter was set up in 1966 with Jim Fleming as President. Ballymena is ultra-conservative in its protestantism, and many were horrified to see Jim 'going pentecostal'. When they eventually realised that the FGBMFI accepted Roman Catholics into their Fellowship they believed Jim had really gone beyond the pale.

Jim's first experience of becoming involved with Catholic charismatics was in 1973. Two girls and a boy from Dublin, all from a Brethren background, told him how they had received the baptism in the Holy Spirit and out of this had come a prayer fellowship in their home. Would men from the FGBMFI come to Dublin and see how the Holy Spirit was moving in that city? Today, Jim Fleming laughs at himself as he remembers going with four or five others one night to the Eustace Hall, a Quaker meeting place in Dublin. Ready to make a quick getaway just in case, he sat right at the back in a corner. He recalls two girls, one a lecturer and the other a barrister, leading the singing. He closed his eyes, listened and thought, 'They are worshipping the Lord. Is this really possible?' It gradually began to dawn on him that maybe God wasn't a Protestant after all! But he was not prepared to go as far as saying that God was a

Catholic either. Thrown into utter confusion, this thought came clearly to his mind: 'These people are worshipping Jesus, and if he hears them and he hears me, but I do not believe they can be worshipping him, then I have a problem. Either my theology is wrong or he is wrong.' Jim is so grateful that he did not close his heart to what the Lord was doing in that place. Many people that night shared their testimonies. Although the terminology and sometimes the theology was different, he knew they loved Jesus.

God was also preparing the ground in the South of Ireland for the day when both sides of the border would come together as one in Jesus Christ. A young Catholic woman called Marie Dowling came to those same meetings in the Eustace Hall in early 1977. She had given her heart to the Lord towards the end of 1976. The meetings were held on Friday evenings at 8 pm, but because of the numbers attending, the doors were shut by 7.15 pm. Marie was anxious for her husband, Denis, to experience salvation, and eventually he was persuaded to come with a friend who was a banker. Denis was outraged by the behaviour of these adult people, raising their hands in the air and praising the Lord. Although it was easy enough for him to close his mind to this, he could not dismiss the testimony of two people who shared specific miracles that God had done for them.

Denis had just become involved with a new company, and because of the circles he moved in he had no wish to come along to these kinds of meetings. However, he did go to a second meeting where a man called Charles Lamb, a Quaker, gave him a book entitled *Love Is an Open Door*. The story was of an American businessman who had retired from a big corporation and opened his home to children with problems. Something in this story touched Denis and he decided to go again the following week. This time Charles gave him a book that was to revolutionise his life. It was entitled *The Happiest People on Earth*. Denis read it at one sitting, crying all the way through it as it moved him as nothing else in his life had ever done. As soon as he had finished the book, Denis phoned Charles to ask him where the local chapter met, explaining that he felt drawn to the Fellowship in a way he could not describe. When Charles told him that there was no chapter in the Republic of Ireland, Denis' response was 'there will be'.

Shortly after this the family went on holiday to Spain where, after listening to a lady preach, Denis committed his life to the Lord. Within two weeks of being home, Charles Lamb phoned to ask Denis and Marie if they would go with him to an FGBMFI convention in Scotland. After their holiday in Spain they had no funds, and because Denis worked in a partnership it seemed unfair to arrange another holiday so soon. However, Marie had some money put by and so they agreed to go. The week they were to go, their solicitor contacted them about a property he had sold for them. He gave them a discount on what they owed, which paid for the trip.

For Denis and Marie, the Scottish convention was an incredible experience. There were not many Roman Catholics, but there were Scottish Presbyterians, Methodists, Anglicans, Baptists and Charles who was a Quaker. The only words Denis could use to describe the atmosphere when they walked in were, 'It was like liquid love.' He had never known anything like this and had an inexplicable sense of moving towards a destiny. On the second night Denis went forward when the appeal was made. Bob Spilman, now an International Director, laid hands on him and immediately he spoke in tongues, his joy knowing no bounds.

On the Friday of the convention there was a men's luncheon. Denis had lost track of Charles, so he found a table at the right of the rostrum where there were two empty seats. He took one and the other was soon taken by a grey-haired gentleman with a very brown, weather-beaten complexion. By his conversation he was obviously from the United States. This man was thrilled to hear Denis share what the Lord had done in his life and asked if he could pray with him. 'I really believe the Lord has a word for you,' he told him, and on a piece of paper he wrote 'Deuteronomy 28:1–28' and signed his name, 'Demos Shakarian'. Denis could not understand why this man had taken the seat next to him when he could have been sitting at the top table, but when he read those verses of Scripture, a whole new dimension of spiritual life opened up to him.

While in Glasgow at a Quaker meeting, Charles met a couple who had been told by God to go to the meeting as there would be a man there to whom they were to give a sum of money towards the work of the Lord in Ireland. As Charles related this experience to Denis and Marie, they sensed that this was God's rubber stamp of approval on opening up a chapter in Dublin.

God is so wonderful in the way he confirms his word. On returning home from Scotland there was an envelope from the Inland Revenue containing a cheque for £300. Not only was God proving that special word to Denis, but it was the dawning of the realisation that they were now walking in the King of kings' supply.

Charles and Denis decided to hold a meeting as soon as possible with some other men whom they knew only vaguely, to pray about how they should go forward. One of the men told them how his business had been on the verge of going into liquidation that very week. After he had prayed, two men came to see him. They had been looking at the business and were interested in buying in or buying it from him provided he wanted to sell. In Glasgow similar testimonies had been given by Americans, Canadians, Scots and many others, but Denis knew that the local men of Ireland needed to experience and share such testimonies in their own community.

'A sense of destiny', conceived in Glasgow, was about to be brought to birth in the South of Ireland. Men from the FGBMFI in the North—Hector Crory, Jim Fleming, George Allen, Billy Burke and others—came together with their brothers in the South. In that country Catholics and Protestants have been on different sides of a great divide for just over four hundred years, but these men were welded together by the Holy Spirit for the work of the Gospel.

The men decided to hold a pilot dinner to see how things went. Many of these men from the South had never stood up in front of people to share their testimonies before. The fact that their knees were knocking and they didn't have the correct terminology was unimportant. What mattered was the tremendous anointing of the Holy Spirit which they experienced, enabling people to be saved and healed. They were so enthusiastic after this dinner that they decided to hold a small convention at the Royal Marina Hotel in Dunlaoghaire. Four or five hundred people came and there were words of knowledge and miraculous healings. It was all totally beyond their understanding. The Lord was using them, in marvellous ways.

This move of the Holy Spirit had an immediate effect in the community. Just a few weeks after returning from Scotland, Denis Dowling heard that his sister, who was five months' pregnant, had been taken into hospital with appendicitis. Marie clearly felt that they must go and pray for her but Denis said he was too busy. Nevertheless they went, Denis hoping that she would be in a private ward. Not only was she in a large public ward, but there were not even curtains around the bed. They asked her if she would like them to pray with her and she agreed. At that moment Denis felt acutely embarrassed but this was immediately followed by an awareness that the Lord was just asking him to be obedient. There was, of course, a hush over the whole ward as they held hands and prayed, and a few minutes later she fell asleep. The following day all the pain had gone, the infection had cleared up, and the doctors who were certain that she would lose the baby confirmed that everything would now be all right.

Denis and Marie did not only experience healing in their family. At this time Denis was secretary of the Equipment Hirers' Association. At one of their meetings a man said that his General Manager was suffering from bone cancer. They were prepared to spend a lot of money to fly a specialist in to see him, but they had been told that the cancer was too far advanced. They were reluctant to send in a priest to pray as the man would then know he was dying. However, at the second dinner of the Dublin chapter a man called Andy O'Neill spoke. He was an insurance official who had spent some time visiting in hospitals. Denis asked if Andy would go with him to pray for this man and for a week or so his condition improved. Then his boss rang Denis saying that he was getting worse again and what was Denis going to do about it. Later that day Denis went to a meeting where a word from the Lord came saying that someone's friend was dying but that the Lord had sent his word to heal him. So Denis rang the boss and told him not to worry any more because the Lord had spoken and healing had already taken place. The man learned the cause of his illness from someone and he began to deteriorate so rapidly that when Denis went to see him he did not recognise him. Nothing daunted, he gave him a copy of *The Happiest People on Earth* and told him that God had spoken and said he was already healed and that he could either believe it or cheat himself by not accepting. He accepted and the Lord healed him completely.

After the Dublin, Limerick and Waterford chapters (which all began about the same time) had been going for a year, all the men felt it right to hold an All-Ireland Convention in the Burlington Hotel, Dublin. Again, men from both North and South came together. Although those from the North knew the Scriptures so well, somehow the Holy Spirit stamped himself as being the authority in those meetings. One very special night, when they were having a time of worship before the Lord in Newry, it was as if the room was full of angels. A word from the Scriptures was spoken out: 'For he is our peace, who has made us both one and has broken down the middle wall of partition between us.' This was exactly what the Lord was doing in this land which knew only too well the meaning of the word 'partition'.

At one of the planning meetings for the convention, they were discussing who they should have as speakers. George Allen tried to phone Demos Shakarian but couldn't get hold of him. At the following meeting they learned that while George had been trying to get through to Demos, he had been trying to contact George. Demos was in a convention where a man had stood up and said that the Lord had told him that something wonderful was going to happen in Ireland and that he wanted to give $10,000 to whatever the Lord was going to do. Demos came over, along with a number of other men from the States, to that first All-Ireland Convention in the last weekend of October, 1978.

One of the most moving moments of the convention was when Al Ryan, President of the Waterford chapter, and Billy McIlwaine embraced on the platform, declaring that Jesus was Lord and it was his love that ruled in Ireland, not the gun. Al was an ex-IRA man with deep family roots in the Provisional Movement and Billy a Protestant ex-paramilitant. Only God could accomplish such a miracle. The press, television and radio commentated on these meetings with the attention usually given to extraordinary events, which of course they were! The five principal Irish dailies interviewed Demos Shakarian, Hector Crory and Al Ryan. Dr Fred Ladenius, the Director of European Publications for the FGBMFI, was interviewed on the radio where he shared that everywhere men were experiencing this renewal and that it was transforming nations as well as individuals. The highlight of the coverage came when *The Late, Late Show*, the most popular broadcast on Irish television, gave Al Ryan, Hector Crory and American astronaut, Charles Duke, the opportunity to speak about the transformation Jesus had brought to their lives.

Looking back, the men smile as they recall their lack of organisational skills, having too many speakers, and the fact that some of the leaders were only just beginning to read the Scriptures. But the Lord was with them. On the last night of the convention, nearly 1,200 people sat down for dinner with another 400 in the overflow area. When the altar call came at the end of the meeting it was as if a great ocean wave of people surged forward. One man who attended this meeting said that he came from a very different denomination from most of those present. For the last fifteen years they had had committees for this, that and the other and had met once a week to ask God when he was going to send his revival to minister to people like those at the convention. 'Then,' he said to these Catholic brothers, 'God turns round and uses a bunch of rookies and we see this colossal wave of people coming into the Kingdom and being set free.'

On the Monday morning following the convention, an Irish Senator came to speak to Demos and Rose Shakarian as they were about to leave. He told them that he had seen reports of the convention on the television and in the newspapers and had attended the banquet meeting. 'I want to tell you,' he said, 'that this group has done more to bridge our people together than anything else that has happened thus far.' Like many others he had seen in action the heart of the Gospel message—love. As Hector Crory expressed it, when he was baptised in the Holy Spirit and came into fellowship with Roman Catholics, he was amazed to find that they had 'the same kind of love'.

6

In the Fullness of Time

Looking back to those early days of the Fellowship, in the late sixties and early seventies, it is difficult to conceive that of the three remaining groups, only Belfast and Ballymena knew of each other's existence. Both were totally unaware of the chapter in Preston, while Preston thought it was the only chapter in the country.

Sadly, the London, Southampton and Birmingham chapters had closed down, the first two by the end of 1967 or early 1968, and the Birmingham chapter in the early seventies. It is difficult to pinpoint a particular reason. As mentioned previously, there was no structured organisation and therefore a lack of support when local problems arose. However, God continued to move, blessing the three remaining groups as they kept alive the vision of the FGBMFI.

God had inspired two ministers in Glasgow, Pastor McLure and David Black, with the desire to see a chapter of the FGBMFI in that city. David Black had been over to America and met up with men from the Fellowship. In 1972 he invited some of them to come over and tell others about the things God had done through the FGBMFI and in their individual lives. The meeting was held in the Charing Cross Hotel. The guests included Jim Winter, now an International Director, and Jim Faulds, now a Field Representative for the area surrounding Ayr, and President of that chapter. As they listened to men like Cliff Powell and Enoch Christofferson they were filled with enthusiasm and determination to start a chapter in Glasgow.

They had no idea how a chapter should be organised, so they ran it as an exclusive Christian men's club. They met once a month, in the Christian Institute, for fish and chips and fellowship! However, these were very precious times for the twenty or so men involved.

One of the most exciting things for the men of the Glasgow chapter was when Jim Faulds made contact with Cecil Stewart, a Christian businessman he knew in Ulster. Cecil told Jim that there was already a chapter of the FGBMFI in Northern Ireland and that it held regular meetings in the Europa Hotel, Belfast. A group of about half a dozen men decided to go over to Northern Ireland to meet with Hector Crory and Cecil Stewart and it proved to be one of the greatest experiences they had ever known. Soon after this another group came over from America, including some of those from the previous trip, to help the Glasgow chapter become really established as well as to spread the vision further afield.

The Glasgow chapter decided to hire the University refectory for their meetings. By now they had discovered that while the chapter was indeed a men's fellowship, ladies were also very much part of the scene, so they took care to invite them along too. Some of the men visited various churches to invite them to the meetings but were disappointed when so many lacked vision for anything outside their own small corner. The Americans were in the area for about ten days, and Jim Winter recalls that this was the first time he had ever seen laymen placing their hands on the sick and praying for them to get well.

Encouraged by the links forged with the men in Ireland, a group from the Glasgow chapter decided to organise an airlift to America. In September 1974 they went to the Pennsylvania area for three weeks, visiting many chapters as well as the Harrisburg convention. This made a tremendous difference to the Glasgow chapter as they began to realise the function and potential of the FGBMFI. About this time the Americans decided to open an office in Brussels to help the work in Europe and John Andor came over from there to encourage the men in Glasgow. They decided that the chapter should become chartered, that is, officially recognised as part of the FGBMFI. The 'chartering meeting' is used as an opportunity to invite civic and church leaders so that they can see for themselves the purpose of the Fellowship. A special speaker is usually invited to present the charter, a framed certificate. On this occasion Art Nersasian, who was responsible for South American outreach, was invited to perform the honour.

Looking back one can see the momentum gathering pace. The various strands of the Fellowship could be clearly seen up to this point in time as they were few in number, but suddenly many new strands were being woven into the pattern. It was God's time to 'go forth and multiply'. In 1976 the *Voice Magazine* advertised a European convention in Brussels in May of that year. It did not occur to any of the Glasgow men that they should attend, but what did interest them was news that a large team of Americans would be stopping off in Britain for a week or so before the start of the convention.

A number of the Americans went down to England while the rest stayed with Jim Winter in Scotland. Meetings were held in Jim's house every night for a whole week. It was indeed a wonderful time. Jim's wife, Dorothy, recalls how lovely it was to talk deeply with the wives of the Americans. It made her realise that these women had a different sort of Christian life from that which she had seen or experienced. One thing she became convinced of, however, was that if God could touch their lives in this way, then he could also touch hers and those of all the other women in Scotland. By the end of the week, with so many people staying and meetings every night, her friends couldn't understand why she wasn't tired out. The only problem was, she told them, that her feet were hurting. So they prayed with her and all the aches left them immediately!

While God was establishing the work of the Fellowship in Scotland, the men of the Preston chapter were still going on in what they thought was isolation. In 1974 they had become extremely discouraged and were on the verge of closing down the chapter when God spoke and said, 'Hold on, I am going to bless this work in a mighty way.' That night they prayed for the treasurer's wife who was very ill at home, some miles away from their meeting. And the Lord healed her! God has such a wonderful way of encouragement which always comes at the right time.

At this time God was also preparing the heart of a management consultant in Cheshire, Bob Spilman. Bob had been actively involved in church organisations for many years, but he knew there must be something more to Christianity than he had yet experienced. One night, in utter frustration, he stood outside a church and cried, 'Oh God, if this is all there is to Christianity, then it isn't worth it!' The Psalmist says, 'This poor man cried, and the Lord heard him.' A little while later Bob read *Nine o'clock in the Morning* by Denis Bennett (Coverdale House [Kingsway] 1974) and he immediately knew what was missing in his experience—baptism in the Holy Spirit.

Bob had a tremendous concern for this country and a great desire to reach businessmen for God, but he was not sure how to go about it. In 1975, while in Vancouver, a friend invited him to a CBMC luncheon meeting where a Christian man from IBM was to speak. Fully expecting the talk to be about computers, Bob was amazed to hear him simply share about what Jesus had done in his life. He knew immediately that this method of testimony in a non-religious setting was desperately needed in Britain. He shared this thought with his brother, Derrick, who asked him if he had ever heard of FGBMFI. He then gave Bob a copy of *Voice Magazine*. But Bob could see nothing about Britain in it and so he wrote off to America to ask if there were any other groups over here. Early in 1976 he received a Chapter Manual. By then he had contacted a number of men in his area in order to come together and pray.

On 24th April 1976, six men came together in Bob's home to start a chapter, two of whom Bob had never met. They knew nothing about what had happened in Britain concerning the FGBMFI and very little about the Fellowship itself. That night they prayed, 'Lord, we don't want to waste your time or our time. If you want us to go ahead, confirm it and make it clear.' Suddenly, one of the men, Tony Holland, spoke out and said he was sure they had to go ahead with Bob as President and Les Hailes as Vice-President. Peter Yates said he agreed with this, and felt that Bob Nock should be Secretary and Tony Holland Treasurer. There was absolute silence for a moment and then Bob asked the men what they should do next. The reply was, 'Well, you're the President—you decide!'

At that moment the telephone rang. The caller was Phil Israelson, an American, phoning from London. He had come to Britain in faith with two other colleagues from the Seattle chapter. Arriving in London they had not known what to do, so they prayed and then telephoned a man in Northern Ireland who had given them the telephone number of the house in Cheshire where the men were meeting. God's timing is perfect. Bob told them that a chapter had just been set up and they had better come. Little did he know what he was letting himself in for! The arrival of the three—Phil, Lee Gaynor and Steve Lightle—was rather like a mini-hurricane as they walked in brimming over with life and vitality, hugging everyone. It was all very un-British.

Bob's wife, Millicent, did not want the Americans to stay with them at that time as it was their son's birthday, so she told Bob that there was a hotel nearby where they could stay. As she rang the hotel the Lord said, 'You have turned away my servants.' She immediately realised that she had to open up her home to them, and as a result they enjoyed wonderful fellowship together. Since that time she has always supported Bob one hundred percent, believing that the work of the Fellowship is her calling as much as Bob's.

Steve Lightle, an American Jew, certainly does not believe in being in God's 'secret service'. To describe him as exuberant, enthusiastic and on fire for God only just begins to give the picture. He is also very persuasive, so when he said that Bob should go to the convention in Brussels the following month, Bob's protestations of not being able to afford it had not the slightest effect. One thing Steve had learned in his Christian walk was that if God wanted you somewhere, you went.

Some weeks before the arrival of the Americans, the President of the Preston chapter, Allan Jones, had received a letter telling him about the men who were coming and asking him to arrange meetings for them. Having talked to the men in his chapter, they decided that there was no point in the Americans coming as they had no money whatsoever. Allan wrote explaining the situation but somehow that letter got lost in the post. The next thing he knew he was being given a telephone message that three Americans would meet him at the Manchester Piccadilly station the following day. Although Allan did not know until later, that call came the night the Cheshire chapter had been started. There was nothing he could do but go and meet them.

The first thing that Steve Lightle did on meeting Allan was to suggest that they all went for a meal (Steve rarely does anything unless it is preceded by a meal). It was an experience Allan will never forget. The four of them went into a restaurant and in loud and enthusiastic tones the Americans asked God to bless the food. Allan wanted to crawl under the table: he wondered what on earth was happening. That night, however, a meeting was arranged between the men of the Preston chapter and those of the newly formed Cheshire chapter. What a meeting that was. For many of the Englishmen it was the first time they had been really released in praise and worship.

Bob Spilman, Allan Jones, Jim Winter in Scotland, and others decided they would go to the Brussels convention the following month. A miracle was needed for their party. When they arrived at Passport Control, Bob discovered that his passport had expired so they prayed that the eyes of whoever looked at it would not see the expiry date. With perhaps more relief than faith, they were ushered through with no problems.

Down the motorway, in Birmingham, God had prompted another two men to attend the Brussels convention. Dillon Harris, with his wife Sue, had been attending local renewal meetings since 1974 where each time he met a Christian who passed on to him American *Voice* magazines. Like many others, he scanned the pages to see if there was anything happening in his part of the world, but there was nothing about Europe, never mind England. In 1976 he too saw the advertisement for the European convention. At that time he was starting up a new business with his partner, Geoff Crocker, and he knew it was not a sensible time to go. However, they prayed about it and both received an inner conviction that they should attend.

Having enquired as to the cheapest mode of travel, the two men decided to go by car via the Dover-Ostend overnight ferry. They had arranged to take Sue to friends in Kent and to pick her up on their return. It was a dark night and being unfamiliar with the roads in Kent they could not find the place where she was to stay. If they were to have any chance of catching the ferry they knew she would have to go with them. At that stage they had no idea how they were going to pay for her, but they drove hard down to Dover only to arrive too late to board. The ferry was still there, but the gates were closed and officials refused to let them through. Somewhat perplexed by the seeming difficulties, they enquired about the next boat and were told it went to Zeebrugge not Ostend. This was more convenient than Ostend but when the ticket office told them it was a special offer whereby they could take as many passengers as they wanted, they knew God was surely in the business. On top of that it was also five pounds cheaper than the other journey.

Everyone was unanimous in their reactions to that first European convention. Words were inadequate to describe the excitement of being part of those meetings. There were many well-known American speakers but also many ordinary people, and it was often these who touched the hearts of the listeners. During the convention it was announced that there would be meetings for each nationality represented. About thirty people were there from England, Scotland and Ireland, and as Steve Lightle prayed with them, everyone knew without a shadow of doubt that God had called and sent them for a purpose.

Before going to Brussels, the Cheshire chapter had arranged their first breakfast meeting for June. They had never yet attended a chapter meeting and there was virtually no publicity, but 118 people came to that breakfast. As in Ireland, it was led by men with no experience of such meetings, but when we step out in faith God is honour bound to fulfil his word and bless us. Within two months they decided to move the meetings to the Manchester Airport Hotel because of the numbers, and the chapter became like a beacon, with the Holy Spirit drawing men and women from all parts of the country.

Returning to the Midlands, Dillon Harris and Geoff Crocker knew they had to do something, but being unsure as to what, they joined the Cheshire chapter ninety-five miles away. They continued to pray and seek God but all he seemed to say was 'wait'. Then in March 1977, at a time of real frustration, God said it was time to go. The only problem was, they didn't know how. Eventually they organised a dinner in Kenilworth and invited all the high-powered businessmen in the area. About seventy came and Steve Lightle was the speaker. That same evening a local rugby club was holding its annual dinner in the hotel—not the quietest of events at the best of times. On that occasion, however, the FGBMFI meeting was so noisy that the rugby folk were walking in, pints in hand, to see what was going on! At the end of the evening, the men were asked to indicate if they were interested in becoming involved in a Midlands chapter. Not a single man responded. They were all happy to support but only as onlookers.

When God gives an individual a vision it is up to him to get on with it. So it was that Dillon and Geoff decided to go ahead in what they believed was the Lord's time. They heard from George Allen of the Belfast chapter that they had invited an American with a healing ministry to come over to Ireland and Scotland and then travel down to London. So the two arranged a breakfast meeting for the third Saturday in June 1977. Personal contacts were made, advertisements placed in newspapers, and over 100 people booked. On Friday a telephone call came from London where the American visitor was supposed to be speaking at an FGBMFI meeting. The men in Scotland had organised his flight to London, which he duly took, only to disappear. Telephone calls were made back and forth to Ireland where George Allen, a cattle auctioneer, kept having to leave his stand to try and sort things out. Eventually a call to the States confirmed that the man had decided to return home. It was too cold in England—in June! George Allen had said to Dillon, 'If you ever really need me, I'll come.' They did, and he came—on the eight o'clock flight from Belfast to Birmingham and shared a beautiful testimony of God's healing in his life.

At that breakfast there was a man with a heart condition who could hardly get up the six steps to the hall. He went forward at the end of the meeting for prayer. Dillon had never prayed for anyone like that man before and although he didn't know it at the time, neither had George. The following Tuesday morning, the man woke up and knew he was healed. He had previously been unable to get out of bed without help, and when he walked downstairs his wife nearly passed out! He gave his testimony at the next month's breakfast.

Although the opening up of the European Office by the Americans, and the Brussels convention, had had a great effect on the Fellowship in Britain, it was, without any doubt, the Glasgow convention of 1977 that provided the catalyst. Immediately following the Brussels convention, Steve Lightle had been made Director of the European Office. He travelled constantly throughout Britain, encouraging and helping to build up the chapters. Early in 1977 he had been to Africa with Tommy

Ashcraft, International Vice-President of the Fellowship, who suggested they just 'drop' into Britain on the way back. They were met by Jim Winter and the first thing he asked them was, 'Could we not have a convention here in Glasgow?' Such is the character of the two Americans that they immediately decided to go round the hotels to find one that would be suitable for a convention. The remarkable thing was that they had talked previously about such a possibility and God had now confirmed it by giving Jim Winter the idea as well.

Steve Lightle called the men of the Glasgow chapter together and told them he believed God wanted them to arrange a convention. To show his commitment, he placed a sum of money on the table as the first contribution and of course those Scotsmen had no choice but to follow suit. Jim Faulds was asked to chair the committee for the convention. It was to be a British Isles convention, so he went over with Steve Lightle to meet the men in Belfast. Jim was quite relieved to see Steve as he had high hopes that he would be able to tell him how to run a convention, but Steve, over the inevitable meal, admitted he had never run one himself either. He told Jim that as he was a businessman he should be able to cope.

The convention, held in September 1977 at the Central Hotel, Glasgow, was three days of heaven on earth. The variety of speakers truly reflected the international aspect of the Fellowship. From England there was the Rev Trevor Dearing, and from Northern Ireland the Rev David McKee. From the United States came Demos and Rose Shakarian, Earl Prickett and Don Ostrom, President of the Seattle chapter which had done so much to help Britain by sending men and finance. For the convention alone, the men of the Seattle chapter had sent £1,500 to help cover the costs. Dr Fred Ladenius, a former member of the Italian 'resistance' (at the age of fifteen), and Press Secretary to Pope John XXIII came from Italy. Pat Kellard, pastor of a Congregational church in Dorset and also concerned with persecuted churches in Eastern Europe, and the Rev Simon Cameron from Faith Acres in Peterhead, completed the list. They were joined, of course, by Steve Lightle, formerly from Seattle but then living in Brussels, and by the chapter presidents from Peterhead, Ballymena, Belfast, Cheshire, Craigavon and Preston.

The Provost of Glasgow was asked to open the convention, but before he was able to perform that task there was a tremendous time of worship and praise. He then stood up and said that he had opened a lot of meetings, many of them very boring, but he had enjoyed every minute of what he had experienced that night. Throughout those three days, the ministry and the worship were beyond anything most of the people had previously known. God moved in salvation, healing, baptism in the Holy Spirit, and in engendering love for fellow members of the body of Jesus Christ. The organisation of the convention was superb in every aspect, and what is more, it was well documented. Information gathered shows that fourteen different countries were represented and, even more important, thirty-seven different denominations.

One lovely story came out of this convention. Three young men travelled up from Preston by car. When they got to Glasgow they stopped at a police station to ask for directions. They were given help and set off again, but when they stopped at some traffic lights, still uncertain of their route, they prayed while waiting for the lights to change. One of the men turned round and looked to his left where a big black car had drawn up. Sitting inside was Demos Shakarian with another grey-haired man. Believing that God had answered their prayers they followed the car, but it turned sharply into a slip road into the hotel car park, so the men from Preston had to drive round to get onto the slip road and into the car park. They parked next to the black car and went in to enjoy the convention. During the course of that day they met Demos and told him how wonderful it was that God had answered their prayer by bringing him alongside them so that he could lead the way to the hotel. Demos looked puzzled and told them that he had not left the convention that day. They then pointed out the man who had been in the car with him and were told that he was Hector Crory, but he also confirmed that neither he nor Demos had left the hotel. These three young men realised that God had kept his word which promises his children the protection of angels.

During the convention an important workshop was held to encourage the formation of chapters in Scotland. Bill Kettles, a science teacher from Dundee, was one who caught the vision for the Fellowship at that meeting. He was to prove a key figure in the development of chapters, not only in Dundee but also down the East coast of Scotland.

Most of the men who had been in Brussels were there, as were many of the new members and chapter presidents. For each one the time was very special. It was as if God was showing them what he could do with an ordinary man or woman who was willing to be available to him. Everyone went home with a new enthusiasm to begin or further the work of the Fellowship in their area. The last meeting was electric. Demos had never seen 500 people all dancing before the Lord, and as they sang 'Joy is the flag', many in that place had to reassess their opinion of the 'reserved' British.

7

Catching the Vision

What exactly is a chapter? First and foremost it is a group of men from a variety of church backgrounds, each one of whom knows Jesus Christ as his Lord and Saviour, and has experienced or is seeking baptism in the Holy Spirit. When such a group comes together with a desire to start a chapter in their town or area, then a Director or Field Representative, one who oversees a number of chapters, will meet with the men. The vision and purpose of the FGBMFI will be shared and after a time of prayer the interested men will be asked to share their own account of how they became Christians. If it is felt to be the will of the Lord, then four officers will be appointed: President, Vice-President, Secretary and Treasurer. At a later date other men may well be appointed to carry out the various duties connected with the running of the chapter.

It is important to stress that the officers must not be from one particular church or fellowship, so that the chapter cannot be dominated by one denomination. Sometimes the chapter members will meet for prayer for some time before deciding to hold their first dinner or breakfast meeting which is always at a hotel or restaurant. No two chapters are alike, each one reflecting to some extent the personality of the president and officers, though guidelines are laid down for the running of the meetings.

Essentially, these meetings are for outreach to those who as non-Christians would never attend church but would respond to an invitation to go out to dinner with their spouse, particularly if they are being paid for! Members or regular attenders are encouraged to bring their friends who do not know Jesus Christ in their lives or those who need to experience the power of God in a new way. Normally, chapters will hold fellowship meetings during the month for members and, perhaps, wives where they can get to know one another and pray for the chapter outreaches. The financial needs of the chapter are usually met through offerings at the dinner where it is stressed that people must not give that which rightly belongs to their church.

Something very noticeable in FGBMFI outreach meals is the way in which people respond in the ministry time following the main speaker. The atmosphere is relaxed and neutral, not religious, and because people have eaten together barriers are broken down. This informality lends itself to sharing the Gospel. After giving his testimony, the speaker will first invite people to accept Jesus as Saviour, and then invite those who wish to be baptised in the Holy Spirit, or who need healing of whatever kind, to come forward and be prayed for. Dr Paul Jinadu, an evangelist and Bible teacher who travels extensively to preach the Gospel, says there is no easier place to help people make a decision for Jesus than in an FGBMFI meeting. In his opinion more people probably come to the Lord in this setting than anywhere else.

Perhaps the best way to describe a meeting would be to consider the reactions and experience of someone attending a chapter meeting for the first time. In April

1977, Dr Ron McCatty, an osteopath from Bristol, was invited to speak at the breakfast meeting of the Cheshire chapter by the President, Bob Spilman. Knowing nothing at all about the FGBMFI, Ron went up fully expecting to be confronted by a group of grim-faced businessmen. He was quite astonished on his arrival to see a room full of men, women and some children sitting at tables and all talking happily. First of all breakfast was served and then there was a short break for an opportunity to walk around, look at the bookstall and meet other people. Ron, as the main speaker, was invited to the top table with the chapter officers.

Then followed a very lively time of praise and worship and again, while Ron was delighted, he had certainly not expected it. It then appeared as if the chapter President picked one or two people at random to speak about how they had found Jesus and how he was helping them in their business and home life. Ron, as the main speaker, was then invited to stand and tell how he had come to know Jesus and how he had been the motivating force in his life ever since. He recalls it as one of the most exciting times ever spent in ministry anywhere.

At the end of his testimony, Ron made an appeal for people to come forward if they needed to commit their life to Jesus or if they needed healing or ministry in any way. He was surprised at how responsive people were, and as he and other men of the chapter prayed with them, many fell on the floor as the power of the Holy Spirit came upon them. In recent years this has become a more familiar happening in charismatic circles, but it was much less so in 1977. It is a wonderful thing to experience the touch of the Holy Spirit in this way. Most remarkably, people are not hurt but rather experience a tremendous peace and often healing of the body or emotions while laid out under the power of the Holy Spirit. On this occasion many received healing, including a young Dutch lady who was nearly blind and had her sight restored. It was two o'clock in the afternoon before Ron and others had finished ministering.

'I must join this Fellówship' was Ron's reaction to that meeting. Although the Cheshire chapter was 114 miles from his home, he décided to become a member and commuted regularly. The reason? It was not only exciting, but it was a form of outreach which surpassed anything he had ever known. Inevitably, it was not long before he developed a longing to see such a Fellowship started in Bristol and with his wife, Nancy, he prayed that the Lord would give them wisdom to know his way forward. Some time later a chapter was established in Bristol with Ron as President. As with Cheshire, it became a beacon for the South-West and Wales as men from all over those areas came to see what God was doing.

Throughout 1976 and 1977 the Cheshire chapter continued to draw men who, like Ron, Dillon Harris, and Geoff Crocker, were prepared to get up at the crack of dawn on a Saturday morning and travel many miles to that breakfast meeting. On many occasions the men from Scotland, an extremely lively bunch with no inhibitions, would travel down to give their support and vociferous encouragement.

Albert Hodgson, a Doctor of Philosophy in Geology, now a financial consultant, had returned to the North-East after a time in Canada and the South of England. While in the South in 1974 he went to some meetings in Green Street, Mayfair, held by Roy Calvorcorressi of Christian Industrial Enterprises Limited. Here he met Bob Spilman who was at that time the Secretary of CIE.

One day he received a letter out of the blue from Geoff Crocker, inviting him to a FGBMFI workshop at the Manchester Airport Hotel. It was only a few sentences and very to the point, saying, 'I think you will find this very important.' He was not sure how his name had got to Geoff but he decided to go for that first weekend of August 1976. Although Albert had previously been in contact with people who were baptised in the Holy Spirit, he had now settled down into a comfortable middle-class church where nothing was allowed to disturb the established order of things. The workshop was preceded by the monthly Cheshire chapter breakfast meeting where Albert again met Bob Spilman, but this time as President of the chapter.

The breakfast meeting was something of a rude awakening. After the meal a man stood up with an accordion to lead the worship. Now if there was one instrument Albert did not like, it was the accordion. He did not know any of the choruses being sung and could not believe it when people stood to their feet and started clapping their hands. The guest speakers were Steve Lightle and Tommy Ashcraft. When the latter stood up to speak he was, in Albert's opinion, over-exuberant, and to make matters worse he actually cried. 'What sort of fellow is this who cries?' thought Albert. Only later did it occur to him that this man had the compassion of Jesus because he had wept when sharing about men on death row.

The key to the breakthrough, as far as Albert was concerned, probably happened over lunchtime. He was sitting at a table with a lovely man from Blackburn, Ivor Heaton, his brother, and a man who was a deaf-mute. Albert had never seen anybody like the latter participate in a conversation with three others before, but Ivor translated for him. In this thoroughly enjoyable time Albert could not help but notice the love that just flowed out from these men. He had never given or experienced love like that and the Holy Spirit was beginning to work in his heart. In the evening they gathered together again, and as they went into the room, the men from the

Glasgow chapter were there pushing a piano into the middle. Albet was very relieved that at least there would be no accordion.

Making what he considered was quite a concession, Albert stood to his feet during the worship time, the like of which he had never seen before. But he had not bargained for being confronted by Jim Faulds from Glasgow, who came straight out with, 'Brother Albert, I believe you need to be filled with the Holy Spirit.' Almost before he could draw breath, there seemed to be about fifteen men around him and immediately he spoke in tongues. To his own astonishment, however, it did not end there because that night he was also released to dance before the Lord. Every month after that he arranged his business appointments so that he could be down in Cheshire for the breakfast meeting. Driving home afterwards the car seemed to be carried on angels' wings. All the things that Albert had so disliked were now like a magnet, drawing him back again and again.

Albert continued to travel each month to the Cheshire chapter until April 1977 when Bob Spilman asked him if he would be prepared to make the necessary arrangements for the setting up of a chapter in the North-East. A number of men had discussed and prayed about this and all felt that this was the way forward. Albert said he would pray about it, more to get Bob off the telephone than anything else as he was not sure he was the right man. Being very meticulous, Albert always took memos of telephone conversations, and at the beginning of each day would commit everything to the Lord. On this particular day, the third day after the call, it was indeed rather like resurrection day, for it seemed as if a light illuminated the memo of the conversation and a voice said, 'Get on with it.'

Albert immediately made the necessary telephone calls. First he rang the Post House Hotel in Washington, where he knew they should hold the meeting, and as Washington was in the centre of Northumbria, he decided to call the chapter by the name of the county. Next he rang a man who had the equipment and could operate the projector to show the film *Good News America*. Finally he rang Bob to say that everything had been organised and he was sure the film could be available for the meeting. This film showed extracts from the FGBMFI World Convention in 1976 and was used at the initial exploratory meetings to give people some idea of what the Fellowship was about. Out of that meeting in Northumbria, six men came together to form the chapter. One was a Roman Catholic, one was from the Salvation Army, another was a Free Church man, and there was a Methodist, an Anglican and, last but not least, one from the Assemblies of God. Normally one would not find people from such a variety of denominations in the same room together, but here they were, sharing a meal and a common aim—to bring men and women to Jesus.

Their first breakfast meeting was the second Saturday in June 1977. Only twenty-one people came and of those eleven had come up from the Cheshire chapter. The way in which the men of the Fellowship travelled to support each other was a tremendous encouragement. During the meeting a word came, through the wife of a Cheshire member, to say that the Lord wanted to speak to someone with a financial problem. The Roman Catholic man indicated it was him and he was prayed for. At the next meeting he came and shared how within two days he had received an unexpected tax refund which solved their problems. Seeing God move in the lives of ordinary men drew more and more people to the breakfast meetings. The second month there were twenty-four people, all from the surrounding area, and within eighteen months numbers had risen to around eighty to one hundred.

God had also been preparing the ground for a chapter

in London. Back in 1974, in Holy Trinity Church, Brompton, the Rev John Grant, a Lutheran minister from the United States, had been speaking at a series of meetings. One of the members, Rodney Radcliffe, spent some time talking to him and told him that he would be in the United States later that year. Being in personnel management with a large company, Rodney had the opportunity to travel all over the world. Hearing he would be in the New England area, John Grant not only invited Rodney to visit them but also gave him an invitation to a FGBMFI convention in New York. On the second day of that convention, Rodney was baptised in the Holy Spirit and set free in a wonderful way. He was impressed by the ministry and witness of the Fellowship but didn't consider it was something of which he should be a part.

Shortly after his visit to the States, Rodney left his job and joined with another Christian, Michael Bretherton, a recruitment consultant, to form a company offering personnel services. When they started the business, they determined to give their 'first fruits' to the Lord's work, and early in 1976 this was a sum of £500. It was then that Rodney received a letter from John Grant inviting him to go to the European convention in Brussels. Rodney was very moved at the Convention, especially by the testimony of Fred Ladenius. When he returned, he explained to Michael why he felt their money should be used to host FGBMFI speakers at their offices, in order to impart the vision of the Fellowship to businessmen in London.

Their first meeting was held in September 1976, and once again the speakers were Tommy Ashcraft and Steve Lightle. The meetings continued on a monthly basis until the following July, when the money set aside had been used up. Among the men who attended the first meeting were two who were to become leaders in the Fellowship: Steve Jackson, now a Regional Director for London, and Buzz Dulley, now an International Director. Both men had only come to know the Lord earlier that year.

Steve, a quantity surveyor, originally came from the North-East but settled in London after attending university there. He married Sue, a girl from London, and they now have two lovely daughters. Steve is a quiet almost diffident person—one who does not make rash decisions but thinks matters through carefully. He had met Michael Bretherton when he applied for a job in Beirut in 1975, but circumstances had arisen which closed that door and for a while there was no contact between them. Then one Saturday morning in February 1976, Steve felt impelled to open his professional magazine, something he would normally never do on a Saturday morning. His eyes fell on a job being advertised by Michael Bretherton and he decided to phone and arrange a visit.

During their meeting, Steve tried to give the impression that all was going well when in actual fact everything had collapsed around him and he wanted to pick Michael's brains about work prospects. Something seemed to be stopping Steve succeeding in business even though he was doing everything well. Knowing he had just started to attend church again, Michael said, 'Perhaps for the first time in your life you are beginning to take Christ seriously and someone doesn't like it.' While sharing that there was power in prayer the telephone rang and as Michael was speaking he mentioned the names of two men in property development, Michael Fenton-Jones, who was then Managing Director of Commercial Union Properties, and David Pickford, Managing Director of Haselmere Estates. Steve was rather taken aback, especially when Michael proceeded to pray over the telephone, as he realised from the conversation that these men all belonged to the Christian

Business Men's Prayer Chain. What struck a chord in Steve's mind was that he had just read Michael Fenton-Jones' professional career story in the *Chartered Surveyor*, and now to hear that he was involved in this prayer chain brought him to the conclusion that there was much more to prayer than he had realised.

Michael continued to talk with Steve for some time, explaining that there really was a devil, whereas Steve had believed that there was only good and bad in people. Having heard Michael speak about his deliverance from black magic and how the Bible was alive and spoke to him every day, Steve could not refuse when Michael said, 'Can I pray for you before you leave today?' He prayed a very simple, gentle prayer that Jesus would be more real to him from that moment on. And from 5th February 1976 at 1.30 pm, Jesus has become more and more real in Steve's life. Just by way of encouragement to those who may be praying for others, he later learned that their nextdoor neighbours had been praying for them for three years! Later that day Steve told his wife, Sue, about his experience and she too gave her life to Jesus Christ. Both were subsequently baptised in the Holy Spirit, so when Michael Bretherton invited them to come and hear two Americans speaking at his office, they were delighted to accept.

Buzz Dulley had also had contact with Michael and Rodney at prayer meetings they held in their office in Dover Street at lunchtimes. Anthony Cordle had invited him along because he knew Buzz had just completed a Lenten series in his church on ambition, and the members of the prayer group were going to be discussing this subject. Buzz was totally bewildered to the point of feeling desperate. These men talked a different language and their views were quite opposite to those he had put forward. Nevertheless, he kept on going and then in July 1976, at the age of sixty, he gave his life to the Lord.

Like Steve, he was only too keen to go along and listen to what Tommy Ashcraft and Steve Lightle had to share. It was the first time he had ever heard of the FGBMFI and he had never encountered such marvellous testimonies as those shared by these men.

In July 1977 the London group decided it was time for them to make a positive step forward. Knowing that the Glasgow convention was to be held in September they decided to hold a large meeting in a London hotel using some of the convention speakers. They prayed for the Lord's guidance as to the venue and the number they should cater for and they all agreed that the meeting should be held at the Lancaster Gate Hotel for about 500. A number of the men in the group also committed themselves to underwrite the costs which they estimated to be about £4,000. Two-thirds of that money had to be submitted in stages a month before the evening and the Lord enabled the right amounts to be available at the right time.

Despite much prayer and many contacts, a week before the meeting only seventy reservations had been made. On the actual evening however, 540 people were present, forty of them American guests. Demos Shakarian was the main speaker but other men gave their testimonies and the people saw God move in a wonderful way. For many it was the first time they had seen businessmen in pin-striped suits praising the Lord. As a result of this and two further breakfast meetings, a London chapter was again established in January 1978.

Lancaster Gate was significant not only for London. Three men from Bath—David Brayton, David Wyatt and David Cook—had earlier been to the Cheshire chapter and decided to attend the Lancaster Gate meeting. They also took with them another man, Don Latham, now the Deputy Chief Executive of Avon County and International Director of the Fellowship.

They set off straight from work and, after the most amazing drive, arrived at the hotel at 7.15 pm. After the meeting David Brayton was full of enthusiasm and insisted that they must have a chapter in Bath. But Don, still a 'respectable' Christian thought to himself, 'If David wants to do it, then he can.' One of David's abilities is to get things off the ground—he is very much a doer and a goer. With Don in tow, he scoured Bath for a hotel where they could have a meeting. They finally decided to have an introductory meeting at the Pump Rooms and see who came along.

David wanted to book coffee for 250 people but Don thought that this was going over the top. He eventually persuaded David to book for 150, but on the night over 250 people came. Allan Jones and Bob Spilman came down and showed the film *Good News America*. In spite of the terrible quality of the film, eighteen men were willing to help start a chapter and every one of them is still in the Fellowship today. Soon after this, Bob and Allan came to organise the setting up of the chapter. Don was appointed as chapter President.

At this point, Don was going through a very difficult time in his Christian experience, but a week previously, the Lord had given his wife, Hilary, a verse of scripture: 'Do not fear: speak out, for I have many men in the city.' After a time of prayer at the formation meeting, Allan Jones repeated exactly the same words to Don, going on to say, 'I, the Lord, have given you the keys of the city.' The first chapter meeting was held in Fortt's restaurant. Numbers between 100 and 150 were the norm, and the Lord blessed them in wonderful ways.

The year 1977 was probably more significant in the history of the Fellowship than even 1965. As we have seen, although the airlift had an immediate and dramatic impact it was not sufficient to provide an ongoing impetus, perhaps because of the lack of Spirit-filled men in the churches. In 1976, the Cheshire and Peterhead chapters were added to the four existing ones in Belfast, Ballymena, Preston and Glasgow. Seven more chapters were opened in 1977, fourteen in 1978, and twenty-eight in 1979, making a total of fifty-five. In that year, at a convention in Blackpool, Albert Hodgson was approached by Gerry Farrel from Dublin and Geoff Sturgess from Wales about their desire to provide Allan Jones and Bob Spilman with new cars. (Allan and Bob were travelling hundreds of miles for the Fellowship, setting up chapters and encouraging those already established, and neither of them possessed a reliable car.)

Albert felt strongly that it was right for the Fellowship to meet this need. Allan Jones had recently spoken at the Northumbria chapter and the following morning he had to call out the AA to start his car. The day after Albert returned home from the convention, there was an announcement that VAT was to go up on the 1st July from 8% to 15% which would increase the price of the cars they had in mind by £500 each. He had planned to write to all the chapters asking them to donate whatever they could, but there was no time for this if he wanted to beat the deadline. He rang Gerry and Geoff but it quickly became apparent that they had no money for such a venture.

Being in his own business, Albert had some savings put by in case of any problems and to him this was his security. He had not yet come to the place where he saw the Lord as the source of all he needed. The amount of money he had was £7,300, and as he prayed it suddenly became the easiest thing in the world to sign the cheque. He was also able to add some extra to make up the full amount. When he had done this he experienced a sense of complete peace in his heart. What makes this even more remarkable is that the first six months of 1978 were the worst he had known in his business—in February he had only earned £68. However, the moment he signed the cheque he knew he was totally free from the bondage of money. Albert says that what the cars did for the Fellowship is nothing compared with what they did in his life! In subsequent years he has experienced the wonderful truth that God is no man's debtor.

The Fellowship was tremendously blessed because men were prepared to sacrifice not only their money but their time and energies. As Bob Spilman and Allan Jones travelled up and down the motorways they would claim the names of the towns they saw on the signposts and see, by faith, chapters established there. In 1980 thirty-seven new chapters were opened, and in 1981, 1982 and 1983, over thirty chapters were established in each of those years. The vision of winning men and women for Jesus Christ, of providing a means of fellowship, and of helping to bring a greater unity in the body of Christ was at last coming to pass.

However, the FGBMFI, like every other Christian group, experiences disappointments and setbacks. Some chapters have had to close temporarily for a number of reasons. Guildford chapter, for example, closed in 1980, having been operating for three years, because there were not enough men giving support. It was reactivated again, but in 1982 the Walton and Weybridge & Farnham chapters were opened leaving Guildford once again lacking in support. On a number of occasions new chapters have been opened too quickly. If the opening of a new chapter means the closing down of another, it poses the question as to whether the time was right. It may be, however, that other towns are better able to support a chapter for a variety of reasons. Sometimes it is difficult to find a good hotel, particularly in smaller towns where choice of venue is limited. One small town in the North has had to suspend its dinner meetings for precisely this reason. The only hotel in the town does not provide meals of an acceptable standard and the same applies to the only restaurant just outside the town. The chapter is trying to overcome the problem by moving the dinner meetings to different villages within reasonable travelling distance.

A chapter can close for the best of reasons. The Cheshire chapter which met for several years at the Manchester Airport Hotel, closed after ten years in 1986. For a long time it had drawn people from all over the country, but so many other chapters have now been opened all over the country and in surrounding towns—Knutsford, Alsager, Northwich (Vale Royal), Salford and Manchester itself—that it has fulfilled its special purpose.

The factor of timing is so important. When full of enthusiasm to see the Lord's work grow, it is easy to run ahead of him. Some chapters may be opened but the right men are not available. When this happens the chapter struggles and it may be necessary to put it into abeyance until the right men come along. There are times when the local churches fail to support the chapter. While the Fellowship aims to reach non-Christians, it is absolutely essential to have the support of mature Christians from the whole range of churches. However, the chapters have not always done their part in informing ministers about the role and aims of the FGBMFI. Consequently, many clergy have either not heard about the Fellowship or have misconceptions about it. It is up to the local chapter to clear up any ignorance or misunderstanding.

In some areas of the country the relationship between the chapters and clergy is excellent. In the Norwich area a booklet containing ministers' views and comments on the FGBMFI has been put together to show how well the Fellowship and churches can work together to their mutual benefit. Many clergy say how the FGBMFI has been such a blessing to them individually and their congregations. Pastor Llewelyn Jones of the Evangelical Free Church, Poringland, tells of the joy it has been to meet people of various denominations. The Rev David Broome, Anglican Vicar of Stoke Holy Cross, Norwich, says, 'The FGBMFI has helped me and my people. Both my church wardens and several church councillors have benefited by attendance at the dinners.'

The Rev John Stride, an Anglican minister in the Dereham Group in charge of Hockering, Honingham, East and North Tuddenham, expresses in an amusing way how many clergy, and laymen, react when first hearing about the FGBMFI:

> California has produced more religious cranks, oddball organisations and curious cults than anywhere else in the world. So it is not surprising that I should have misgivings when I came across an organisation founded by an Armenian Pentecostal dairy farmer in California. With an origin like that, a name like 'Full Gospel Business Men's Fellowship International', and a record of rapid growth around the world, it hardly looked the sort of thing that a Church of England Vicar in rural Norfolk would want to get involved in.

He does go on to say, however, that that was two years ago and in the succeeding months his misgivings have been sufficiently overcome for him to become a member of the Fellowship, albeit through the generosity of one of the national leaders. This year he paid his own subscription and intends to continue to do so, 'and that is a true test of the value I place on FGBMFI'. Rev Stride also says that for himself, his wife and upwards of a dozen of his parishioners, the local chapter of the FGBMFI has been a source of encouragement, challenge and spiritual growth. This is how it should be if chapters are fulfilling the aim of helping the churches and bringing a greater unity to the body of Christ.

Without doubt, the most important reason for chapters closing down is when they fail to catch the vision of what the Fellowship is all about. Its primary aim is to bring men and women to Christ, but at times some chapters lose sight of this and become, in effect, Christian social clubs. When this happens the chapter cannot function correctly because it has lost its reason for being. Proverbs 29:18 says, 'Where there is no vision the people perish.'

8

'100 Not Out'

John Wright, a businessman from Norwich, is a man much used of God in the FGBMFI. He came to know the Lord rather suddenly and dramatically at the age of thirty-two, the time in his life when he thought he had everything except a wife. God met the desires of his heart in that direction eight years later when he married Sue, and they now have five very lively children. In 1977 he was introduced to Bob and Millicent Spilman through a mutual friend, Roy Calvocoressi. As they gave him a copy of *The Happiest People on Earth* to read, both he and they felt that there was a deeper purpose in their meeting than appeared on the surface.

John was gripped by this inspired book as he saw the implication of the vision God had given to Demos. At the first opportunity he accepted an invitation from Bob and Millicent to stay with them and attend a Saturday morning breakfast to see for himself what happened. The result was beyond his wildest expectations. About 120 men and women were seated for breakfast, yet what captured John was not the number of people but the love which seemed to envelop everyone in the room. After experiencing praise and worship of a quality he had never come across before, he was enthralled by the testimonies of three ordinary businessmen who, for just a few minutes, simply described what God had done in their lives. The stories were of physical healing, restored marriages and God's power to provide in times of desperate need—real-life situations to which those present could relate.

The main speaker was Harry Greenwood, an ex-Royal Navy able seaman whom John had met the previous evening for the first time. John freely admits that he dismissed Harry, a large and apparently extrovert man, as 'unspiritual'. He later discovered that Harry's extraordinary sense of humour was a way of compensating for his innate shyness. When he stood up to speak, he confirmed John's worst suspicions as every sentence seemed to contain a wisecrack. But it was a morning for learning lessons. Harry had not been speaking long before John realised that his words came with the power of the Holy Spirit upon them.

During the time of ministry, the Lord gave Harry words of knowledge regarding people's medical conditions and many were manifestly healed by the power of God. A man who hobbled to the front suffering from a slipped disc, danced all the way back to his seat. A lady who was deaf in one ear had her hearing restored. John had been aware of the healing ministry but would never have fully believed had he not seen it with his own eyes.

Driving home down the M6 that afternoon, John sang at the top of his voice and could scarcely contain his excitement. The first thing he did on arriving at his house was to ring a local pig farmer, Alan Pimlott. While at the Cheshire chapter, John had been given Alan's name because he had indicated an interest in starting a chapter in Norwich. Alan's father, Sedley, as well as being a farmer, was also pastor of the Mount Zion Fellowship. John later discovered that he had been praying for ten years that a chapter might be started in their area. Sedley had been to the London convention in 1965 and Alan's wife, Ann, was one of the Cameron family from Peterhead who were involved with the FGBMFI up in Scotland. Sedley and Alan had also been over to the United States and met Demos there in 1967, and so they had had many contacts with the Fellowship.

Alan was very excited when John rang him, particularly when he invited him to lunch. Having heard that John was a former merchant banker and was also a company director, he thought he had better do justice to the occasion. For those who know Alan today, the present model is much slimmer than the one of the 1970s, and he had a reputation for enjoying his food. Arriving at John's office in his smart suit he was more than a little disappointed to discover that for John, lunch was one round of sandwiches and an apple! More importantly, they prayed and decided to get men together to form a chapter.

Their first dinner attracted about 120 people and once again the speaker was Steve Lightle. John recalls being terrified having had no experience of running such meetings, but the Lord carried them through. The chapter was extraordinarily privileged in having Alan Pimlott to lead the worship. There is a tremendous anointing on his ministry and God has been able to use him in this special way all over the world. One retired missionary clergyman travelled the fourteen miles to the dinner on his bicycle and said it would have been worth it just to be part of the worship. He had never heard anything like it in his life.

Within a few months of the chapter starting they moved to the City Suite of the Hotel Norwich, an ideal venue which can take up to 250 people. In April a farm labourer's wife attended one of these dinners, came to the Lord, and was filled with the Holy Spirit. She went home so transformed that her husband came to the May dinner. He made no commitment that night but went away with lots to think about. At the June dinner he too came to the Lord and was filled with the Holy Spirit. They had a six-year-old daughter who had been deaf from birth. When they got home that evening, in simple faith, they took out her hearing aid and said, 'Jesus is going to give you your hearing back.' They prayed for her, sent her out of the room, and then called out to her. She came running in shouting, 'I can hear! I can hear!'

Shortly after the start of the chapter, the Lord began to teach John about money by a very simple method. Their sources of income completely dried up and one week he found himself committed to paying £1,000 by the following Monday without any evident source of finance. John found it difficult to trust God at the best of times, so although he prayed he decided to try and help God out. Some fees were owed to the business and he attempted to get hold of these by Saturday. He called in at the office to see if anything had arrived, but had to admit defeat. He arrived home to find a letter that had come by the lunchtime post. It was from Bob Spilman, who knew nothing of their difficulties, and said, 'Millicent and I have had separate confirmation from the Lord that we should send you the enclosed cheque for £1,000. We don't know what it is for, but we know that you will know, and we praise God.' Stunned by what God had done, John bowed before him and said, 'Lord, when will I ever learn to trust you?'

When he rang Bob that afternoon he was told that they had received an unexpected cheque on the Thursday from an insurance policy taken out twenty years previously, and being in desperate need of a new car, they praised God for his provision. While praying that morning, the Lord spoke to each of them separately and told them to send the £1,000 to John and Sue. Thinking these two had plenty of money, Bob and Millicent thought it made no sense but they were obedient. What a wonderful testimony to God's provision! Not only were John and Sue blessed, but God met the need of a car for Bob and Millicent through Albert Hodgson; and in turn Albert was able to prove that 'God is no man's debtor'. It is also a lesson on how the members of the church of Jesus Christ are dependent upon, and responsible to, one another.

The chapter in Norwich has been used in a similar way to that in Cheshire: first, attracting people from a wide area, then encouraging men to begin chapters in their own towns. So it was that Ipswich, Yarmouth and Diss were started as a result of Norwich. Many clergy in this area have spoken about the encouragement the FGBMFI has given them as individuals and to men in their churches. They see the Fellowship as being a tool for evangelistic outreach whereby men and women are then brought into the churches. It is also a means of ministering to clergy who find themselves constantly giving out, for in chapter meetings they can enjoy fellowship and receive for themselves.

God uses many different ways to get our attention when he wants to move in our lives. For Bert and Pauline Sture of Bradford, it was a visit to Bert's brother in Canada in 1976, as a way of celebrating their twenty-fifth wedding anniversary. Bert's brother, David, invited him to go to a men's 'advance' in Ontario where he was to be one of the speakers, on the subject of the baptism in the Holy Spirit. This was Bert's first contact with the FGBMFI, and although he went with a limited amount of faith, he saw miracles not only in other people's lives but also in his own. Bert had been brought up in a Christian home and attended a Pentecostal church all his life but he felt dry and empty. Just before his wedding, he had a serious motorbike accident which left him with one leg shorter than the other and constant pain for the next twenty-five years. In one of the meetings the Lord met him spiritually and physically. The Holy Spirit touched him powerfully and the pain in his leg, caused by crippling arthritis, went for good.

When they returned to England, Bert prayed that he would never be the same half-hearted Christian that he had been for so long: he wanted spiritual reality. He had no idea that there were any chapters in Britain, so when his brother David came over the following year and brought a *Voice Magazine* advertising the Glasgow convention, he knew it was right to go. Never before had he heard people singing in tongues as they did in those meetings—it sounded like a heavenly choir. Hearing of the Cheshire chapter, Bert and Pauline went over, taking two friends with them. Pauline was particularly impressed by the way Bob Spilman was directed by the Lord in leading the meeting.

Allan Jones was given Bert's name as a contact because as yet there was nothing in Yorkshire, and when the next chapter list was sent out, to his surprise, Bert found his name officially listed. Greatly encouraged by Allan, the Bradford chapter held its first breakfast in March 1978. Again, it became a centre, attracting men and women from all over Yorkshire and the borders of Lancashire, and they learned much about how to minister in the Spirit, to live lives of faith, and the blessings of giving. It has spawned many chapters in surrounding areas, including Halifax, Batley, Skipton, Hebden Bridge and Leeds.

In 1978 it was thought that Leeds would be the next obvious place to have a chapter, but whatever moves were made seemed to be blocked. There were difficulties in finding a venue as well as strong opposition. In 1983, five years after first trying to establish a chapter in Leeds, the men of the Bradford area felt it right to hold a one-day convention there. At a Directors' meeting shortly after this decision, a word of prophecy came through one of the men to Bert that he should go in and possess the city. They had gone round it seven times—figuratively speaking—in prayer, and it was now open to them. It was a wonderful day when God moved in many lives for salvation and healing, and the convention was an encouragement to the newly formed chapter.

Coincidences are something most people accept, but when one comes into a vital, living relationship with Jesus Christ, he is able to speak to us by what many Christians call 'God-incidences'. These are when circumstances are such that it would be more difficult to disbelieve in God than to believe. Near Bert Sture's home is a newsagent whose son, Warren, has a friend in America. This friend wrote to him, giving him the name and telephone number of someone in his area who was involved in the FGBMFI and encouraging him to get in contact. The name and telephone number was that of Bert who lived only 200 yards away from Warren. That young man went to a breakfast meeting in Bradford where he came to know the Lord and was baptised in the Holy Spirit. Since then he has witnessed so openly that many of his family and colleagues have also come to know Jesus Christ.

Canada was the place for yet another man from the North to make contact with the Fellowship. George Harper, originally from the North-East but now living with his wife Doris in York, went over to Calgary in 1978. George had not long since come to know the Lord and he was happy to accept an invitation from a friend to attend a breakfast meeting. In his words, that meeting 'blew his mind' and he longed for something like it in England. While in the meeting, someone came over and prophesied over George and Doris. This was only the second time in their life that they had heard prophecy, the first time being just a few months before in a meeting in England when someone they did not know came and prophesied over them. What was even more remarkable was that this second prophecy was a confirmation of the first one.

Later that year, George was in a Baptist church in Tyneside, talking to his brother-in-law, when a deacon happened to mention he had been to a breakfast meeting in the Post House Hotel at Washington. As a result of that conversation he started to attend the Northumbria chapter breakfasts from early 1979. It was different to anything he had experienced in this country and he began to sense that something was happening to him and for him. At the Blackpool convention in May that year, Albert Hodgson asked George to try and get men together in York. But George delayed for a year, thinking that he didn't know enough people to ask and that it needed a 'great man of God' to organise such things. He spent the time looking for 'spiritual giants' but not finding them.

In 1980, Doris went to a meeting in York Minster to hear Juan Carlos Ortiz and the following night persuaded George to go with her. At that meeting they met John and Sue Pearson who mentioned that they were involved in setting up a chapter of the FGBMFI in Northallerton and invited George and Doris to their first meeting. Finally persuaded that God could use ordinary people, George arranged a meeting, as a result of which the York chapter came into being in September 1980. They saw God move in salvation, particularly the night when the Rev Eric Townson spoke and twelve people out of the seventy there, committed their lives to Jesus Christ. The Charter dinner was also quite outstanding. Allan Jones was the speaker on that occasion and while he was sharing his testimony, the wife of the Treasurer, Christine Mitchell-Innes, was healed of arthritic lumps on her wrist—they just disappeared.

1980 also saw the North Humberside chapter come into being, to cover the area from Hull to Goole. God has worked in a wonderful way, building up the chapter, sometimes very slowly, but over time barriers of suspicion have broken down as people and clergy have seen God change their lives. One local vicar told the President on one occasion that he was wholeheartedly in support of the Fellowship. Knowing that this man had never been to a dinner meeting, the President asked what he meant. The vicar said that one of his most faithful and hardworking church members was a lady who became a Christian in an FGBMFI meeting. She had only been to the one dinner but her life had been radically changed. Like the York chapter, North Humberside has seen God move mightily in salvation. On one occasion when Allan Jones was speaking, ten out of fifty people gave their lives to Christ, and on two occasions when Professor Roy Peacock was the speaker, a similar number made decisions. There is nothing more stimulating to one's Christian faith than to see men and women coming to know Jesus, and it is now unusual for a dinner to go by without at least one person making a commitment.

Most chapters experience some difficulties from time to time, but generally those chapters which look outwards to extending the work are the ones which grow and see God's blessing. Those who do this find that although their core membership is depleted in the short term, God brings in new people to fill the gap until the next chapter is opened. Don Latham in Bath felt that they should be looking towards Trowbridge and Chippenham for chapters in those towns, but as they only had about twenty members, he wanted to hang on to them. One day he was at a meeting in Ron McCatty's house with a number of men when Dillon Harris prayed in faith, 'Lord, thank you for the chapters in Trowbridge and Chippenham.' Don then knew he had to let go of the concern about membership and trust the Lord. The Bath chapter has now been responsible for starting at least seven other chapters and their own membership has grown every time, not diminished.

One of the areas the men in the South-West were looking to was the Isle of Wight. David Brayton from Bath came into frequent contact with a solicitor on the island and he kept him supplied with *Voice* magazines. Gradually, David came across quite a number of people there who had experienced the charismatic renewal, so when his solicitor friend, Clive Rolfe, said he thought that the time was right to start a chapter, they arranged a meeting. David, Don and Buzz Dulley went to this meeting where eighty men were gathered together. After talking about the Fellowship, they asked how many men would be interested in joining and supporting a chapter—and forty stood up! It was impossible to ask all forty men to give their testimonies, as is the usual procedure, so Buzz asked each of them to write their names on a piece of paper. He then spread them out in front of him and said, 'Will you pray, and we will ask the Holy Spirit to show us who should be the officers as we do not have time for hearing all your testimonies.' It was as if the papers lit up. Buzz then read out the names of the men they believed the Lord had indicated to them and asked all those present to say if they felt an inner witness of the spirit that their choice was right. All the men confirmed that the choice was indeed right, and the officers of the chapter were duly appointed.

Just over the border from Devon lies the small Cornish town of Callington. Terry Waters, one-time Mayor of Callington and a well-respected businessman in Plymouth was introduced to the Fellowship when Allan Jones was invited to speak at his church. Having been a Gideon for many years, he was concerned to reach his fellow businessmen for Christ. As he says, the vision of FGBMFI really grabbed him and he knew that God wanted him to help start a chapter in the city in which he worked. Their first speaker was Lee Buck from the United States. Terry recalls that they had no idea how to organise things in the 'right' way but God wonderfully blessed that meeting and many people came to know the Lord.

One of the most amusing incidents in the early years of the Plymouth chapter was when Ron McCatty came over from Bristol to speak at their meeting. As always, they had a time of worship and then the main speaker. After giving his testimony, Ron received words of knowledge from the Lord regarding individuals in the room. As they responded to these and Ron prayed, usually without even putting his hands on their head, they fell down under the power of the Holy Spirit. Suddenly, the managers of the hotel knocked at the door, their faces showing great concern. 'We're not insured for this kind of thing,' they said. Terry then explained to them that the people were not ill, quite the reverse, God was healing them.

Men of the FGBMFI were certainly going out and 'possessing the land'. The first London chapter had been given a vision that they would become a beacon to men in the surrounding areas who would initially be drawn to their chapter meetings and then start chapters in their own areas. Although that did not come to pass in the 1960s, a decade later saw Woodford, Luton, Croydon, Wimbledon, Richmond, Heathrow, and the City of London chapters. A great impetus was given when the officers of the London chapters felt it right to hold a European convention in the Wembley Conference Centre from 27th to 30th August 1980. Much prayer went into the decision as to the city and venue, but it was felt that London had a strong Fellowship to support a convention, and the Wembley Centre was well equipped for such an event with many rooms and restaurants and an auditorium that could seat 2,700 people.

Financially, it was a tremendous venture of faith. Expenses for the use of the building alone were £17,000 to which had to be added the cost of brochures and advertising, speakers' expenses and a film company to make a video. The final budget was estimated at £32,000. As they had done so often in the past, members of the Seattle chapter in the USA sent a generous gift of $2,500 to help towards expenses. The theme of the convention was 'Jesus Triumphant', expressing the desire to uplift the name of Jesus. The many testimonies given over those few days certainly did that. The writer well remembers the almost tangible sense of the Lord's presence. When hands were raised in praise and worship the whole atmosphere was charged with the power of the Holy Spirit.

Perhaps the most moving moment of the convention came when Don Ostrom, President of the Seattle chapter, asked for men to come forward, first those who wanted to be baptised in the Holy Spirit and then those who would be willing to serve the Lord and travel for him in Europe. It was a wonderful sight to see hundreds of men standing together at the front of that auditorium, some praising God and many weeping, aware perhaps of what God might demand of them. The fruits of that meeting have been seen over the last few years as men from Britain and Ireland have gone out in small groups or airlifts, almost always at their own expense, to fulfil the great commission.

The promotional video *You Shall Be My Witnesses* was to a great extent made during the convention, some additional filming being done in the Norwich area. Demos Shakarian, the speaker at the final meeting, briefly tells how God brought the Fellowship into being, stressing that the FGBMFI is not a church and nor has it ever been intended to become one. Also interviewed is the Bishop of Pontefract, the Right Rev Richard Hare, a popular speaker at FGBMFI meetings. He endorses Demos' statement and adds that in his opinion, the men who are involved in the Fellowship are often those who are most involved in their local churches. Bob Spilman describes the aims of the Fellowship and others testify to the way their lives have been changed since being invited along to a meeting.

Directors and officers involved in organising the convention learned much from their experience. One thing was that they overestimated the number of people who wanted meals. This left a rather large deficit. Many chapters and members responded to the need but most unexpectedly, the brothers in Canada, hearing of the problem, sent thousands of dollars to clear the major part of the deficit. It truly was an expression of 'brotherly love'.

Wembley had much the same effect as the Brussels and Glasgow conventions in that faith was built up, enabling chapters to become more outward looking, and thus the work grew. Two national conventions had been held at the Norbreck Castle Hotel, Blackpool, in 1978 and 1979. Both were a tremendous blessing. As a result of all these conventions, regions as well as individual chapters were inspired to hold one and two-day conventions where members could share their testimonies and hear Bible teachers from many denominations.

The June/July 1981 edition of *Renewal* magazine carried an article entitled '100 Not Out'. Written by Bob Spilman, it described the expansion from six chapters in 1976 to a hundred in February 1981. *Renewal* described the FGBMFI as one of the fastest growing organisations in Britain at that time. Bob described the Fellowship in the following way:

This is a laymen's fellowship which includes men from all church denominations and backgrounds, but with the common bond that they love Jesus. Usually the members of the fellowship are baptised in the Holy Spirit or, if not, are seeking to be thus empowered to be witnesses for Christ. So the fellowship is a natural follow-on and continuation of the work God started through Fountain Trust and other renewal groups during the 60s and 70s. The members of the fellowship are not only concerned with enjoying fellowship with each other, but also with working together to reach others with the gospel message and to destroy the works of Satan.

9

'Better than Walking on the Moon'

God had not forgotten the 'land of revivals'. In 1958, David Greenlow from Ireland gave an American *Voice Magazine* to Gwylfa Richards, living in Swansea, South Wales. He was tremendously impressed, and took out a subscription to receive a copy every month, and also sent for tapes from the conventions. Then in 1965 Enoch Christoffersen corresponded with Gwylfa in an attempt to start a chapter in Swansea. The Americans thought that South Wales was just like another American State and all they had to do was find a local hotel and everyone would turn up. There were a number of men locally who had heard great things about the Fellowship, but it seemed that cultural differences held up the beginnings of the work in that part of the country. However, God moved in his time.

In 1977, Gwylfa's daughter Bethan went to Norwich for the Zion Fellowship Convention, and while washing up one night with a man called Allan Jones from Lancashire, she heard about the Fellowship and the forthcoming convention in Glasgow. Her father and brother-in-law decided to go, and on their return they again attempted to begin a chapter but men were reluctant to commit themselves. For about a year after this, four men prayed together regularly, and their times of prayer were so powerful that they knew something would happen. One night a man came to join with them. His name was Walter Wainwright and he had been involved in the first Birmingham chapter. He was able to tell the others much more about the Fellowship so that when the next step came they were ready to take it.

Throughout this time, Allan Jones would phone Gwylfa and ask him what was happening to which the reply was always that they were praying. But in 1979 they had a telephone call from Canada asking if they could bring a party of men over to Wales. Because of problems with accommodation, only six came and of these some stayed in the South and West and two went over to Newport where God had prepared two men, Richard Sheppard and Ray Pollard. Richard was running his own furniture warehouse and Ray was an ex-light heavyweight boxing champion.

While at a big crusade meeting in 1978, Richard heard a word of prophecy for him through the visiting speaker who was from California. God said that Richard would be involved in another business where many souls would be saved, but Richard did not understand at that time what God meant, only that it was for him. A month later he went on holiday to Gibraltar and a lady gave him a copy of *The Happiest People on Earth* to take with him. For the first time in his life, Richard actually read a book right through.

A month after his holiday, a pastor friend from Bristol phoned Richard to say that a group of businessmen were meeting in a hotel in Bristol for breakfast and he thought Richard might be interested. Richard and Ray are almost inseparable, so the two went together. They were almost put off because of black ice on the roads, but they prayed and decided to trust the Lord and go. Although they came from a Pentecostal background, they were quite taken aback by the freedom in praise and worship, and afterwards they intimated that they would be interested in starting a chapter in Newport.

The remarkable thing for Ray was that he had become a Christian through hearing the testimonies of FGBMFI men. In 1964 the pastor of his church brought an American dairy farmer over to speak. It was, of course, Demos Shakarian. Jerry Jensen was also there and the pastor, Eric Dando, asked him to pray with people for baptism in the Holy Spirit. They took all the new converts out to another room and the first person Jerry prayed for was Ray. Now, Ray was not used to being in church and as far as he was concerned he had gone forward simply to become a Christian, so when Jerry came to lay hands on him he started throwing punches as if he were in the boxing ring. Some of the larger members of the church had to jump on him and hold him down to the ground!

The following year Ray went to the London convention in the Albert Hall and met Demos and Jerry once again. Jerry said he would never forget that night in 1964, particularly as it was the first time he had ever tried to lay hands on anyone. Ray was not impressed by the 1965 London convention. He was convinced that they were all crazy. Not being baptised in the Holy Spirit at that stage, he could not cope with the speaking in tongues and what was rather a noisy atmosphere. Again, God's timing was perfect, for when the time came to set up chapters in Wales, the men were ready, whereas in the 1950s and 1960s that was not the case.

Allan Jones went to Newport in February 1979 to show the film *Good News America*. Over 200 people attended that meeting from a full cross-section of the churches in the town. Their first breakfast was held in May when Andy Milliken was the speaker. Over 100 people came and three local businessmen gave their lives to Jesus Christ.

John Cann, a Welshman who had emigrated to Canada, led the team of men who carried out an almost unbelievable timetable of meetings. They travelled everywhere, going into schools, universities, churches and fellowship meetings for three weeks, and at almost all these meetings people came to know the Lord. Large numbers attended, for example, in Merthyr and Dowlais over 300 people came and the response for ministry was tremendous. Out of this visit sprang the Swansea chapter which started in July 1979 in the Dragon Hotel, and soon afterwards, the Llanelli chapter came out of Swansea.

God showed his power in the Swansea chapter in some wonderful ways. An American, John Turnbull, and his wife were staying at the Dragon Hotel. John, from Indiana, was an executive for ICI. Having no idea that a chapter had started in Swansea, he went down to the reception desk to find out if there were any Christian meetings they could attend and was told that the FGBMFI was holding a dinner in the Dragon that night. A keen member of the Fellowship, John could hardly believe it, and the Lord was able to use him and his wife in healing in ways people had never before experienced.

Another remarkable testimony is that of Ray Lewis. He was headmaster of a large school and in 1979 his wife died very suddenly. Totally devastated, he rejected God and on a number of occasions drove his car down to Mumbles intending to drive over the cliffs, but every time someone came up and spoke to him. Ray and his wife had no children and he felt as if there was nothing left. The President of the Swansea chapter, Ray Samples, was also a headmaster and knew of Ray's difficulties. The men of the chapter began to pray for him. One morning in his local Anglican church, a man asked him if he was Ray Lewis and would he like to come to a breakfast meeting at the Dragon Hotel. Ray agreed to go.

During the week before that breakfast meeting, Ray had shouted out, 'If there is a God, send someone here. If there is no God, I am going to commit suicide.' At that moment there was a knock on the door and a man who lived down the street was standing there. When Ray asked why he had come he said that he didn't really know but he felt that he had to come and talk to him because Ray needed some help. That night this man was able to lead Ray into a new experience of God and to accept Jesus Christ as his Lord and Saviour.

After the breakfast meeting, Ray knew that God wanted him to be part of the FGBMFI. He later remarried and their home became a meeting place for the FGBMFI so that they were able to host many of the visiting speakers to the Fellowship. Like David the Psalmist, Ray can now say, 'This poor man cried, and the Lord heard him and delivered him out of all his fears.'

Phil Jones, who is now President of the Swansea chapter and a Field Representative vividly remembers his first introduction to the FGBMFI. A church colleague took him to a prayer and praise meeting in the hotel where their chapter met. About twenty men were sitting in a circle in this room, but what caught Phil's eye was the banner along one wall proclaiming, 'His Banner over Us Is Love!' Phil was impressed first and foremost by the welcome which was full of love, and also by the sense of oneness and the simplicity, sincerity and faith of their prayers. Phil felt as though he had a crust around him which needed to be broken before he could enter into this kind of worship. He also knew deep down that there was something about this group that he wanted to identify with. That night he went home full of wonder at the Fellowship's lack of formality. He had experienced something very powerful and moving, and he wanted to know more about this Fellowship.

The following month Phil again went to the prayer and praise meeting and this time he was asked to lead in prayer with regard to a particular request. He felt self-conscious, but when he started to pray it was as if the others were lifting him up with their support. Shortly after this Phil went to his first dinner meeting where he heard a Canadian talking about Christ in such a loving way that it created an excitement he could not contain. Phil now knew that there was a yearning within him for a more tangible experience with God, to see in his life what he had heard expressed.

One of the great blessings for the people in Wales was to be invited to the Bristol one-day convention in May 1981. In much the same way as the Glasgow convention and Lancaster Gate meeting had proved important turning points, so this convention fired everyone who attended with a new enthusiasm for the Lord and for winning men and women for Christ. For Phil, the excitement of meeting people so inspired would have been enough to make the day worth while. But during the time of praise he was released in a new way to enter into the worship and realised that he was no longer an onlooker but a participator. The first testimony was given by John Tomlinson from Carlisle, and to Phil's amazement he spoke about receiving experiences from God that very day. In the time of ministry following this, the atmosphere was charged with expectancy, and when they saw how a cripple's feet were healed and his legs grew, they could hardly take it in. At the final evening session the man danced in the time of worship, no longer lopsided and with no trace of a limp!

Ron McCatty and those organising the convention had no idea who should speak at this evening session, so they decided to leave it to the Lord and trust him. Twenty minutes before the dinner meeting was to start, David Willows, evangelist and musician from the Holly Bush Fellowship, came in. Immediately, Ron went over to him and said, 'You are speaking tonight.' Somewhat taken aback, David said he had only just come in but Ron merely replied, 'God has said you are speaking.' That evening meeting was so blessed that for months afterwards Ron received letters from people all over the country saying how the Lord had touched them there.

On a number of occasions the chapters in Wales were privileged to be visited by Ernie Hollands, an exciting speaker from the Fellowship in Canada. An ex-prisoner, Ernie had spent twenty-five years in maximum security jails, the last term being for armed robbery when he shot a policeman. While in prison he made fish hooks and a man called Bailey, who owned a sports shop bought these to sell. Bailey was a member of FGBMFI. He began to pray for Ernie and eventually he visited him. When he told Ernie that he loved him and that Jesus loved him too, Ernie just broke down and cried. He gave his life to the Lord and after that he could hardly wait for the monthly visit. When he was released, Bailey took him to his home, clothed him and gave him a job in his shop—looking after the till. Ernie could not believe that anyone could love him so much and trust him to that extent.

On one of Ernie's visits to Wales in 1982, Ray Pollard met him at Heathrow Airport at 8.30 in the morning. Ernie came through customs clutching suitcases emblazoned with 'Jesus Christ is Lord' and 'Praise the Lord'. His words came tumbling out: 'Praise the Lord! Where's Maidstone prison?' He had contacted the governor and arranged for Ray to go with him. There they visited a man who had committed a very serious offence and was serving a life sentence. The prison officer, with an alsatian dog, brought the man into the room and warned them that their conversation would be listened to. Ernie started talking to this man who asked, 'Do you think I am forgiven?' and Ernie told him, 'Yes, if you know Jesus.'

At the end of their time the prisoner asked if he could see the governor but the officer said that he doubted it. However, the governor did come down and Ernie had the opportunity of sharing his testimony with him. After the prisoner had returned to his cell, Ray was asked if he knew who the man was, but he said that he had no idea. They told him that he was imprisoned as part of a group who had taken part in some horrific bombings, but even the prison officers had to admit that he was now a completely changed man.

Ernie also had opportunity to go into the prison at Swansea. After speaking to the men, eighteen prisoners and three prison officers stood up to indicate that they wanted to commit their lives to Jesus Christ. The Borstal at Usk allowed them to hold a lunchtime meeting, but the governor said it would have to be a voluntary attendance. Fifty-eight men came and at the end of the meeting, every one stood up to accept the Lord into their lives.

The greatest impact that the FGBMFI has had in Wales was probably in 1986 when Charles Duke, the astronaut from the Apollo 16 mission, came over to tour the chapters there. In Newport almost 400 people came for Sunday lunch, including many dignitaries such as the Deputy Mayor and Chief of Police. Charlie, as he is affectionately known, was able to tell them that coming to know Jesus as his Lord and Saviour was 'better than walking on the moon!' Later that day over 600 people gathered from many churches to see his film taken on that mission and to hear his testimony.

Tremendous interest in the Fellowship was created when Charles Duke visited the Swansea area. He was presented to all the civic dignitaries of Swansea, Llanelli and Carmarthen and gave them *Voice* magazines which has now led to them being placed in every council office in Carmarthen. The Mayor and Mayoress of Llanelli were so touched when Charles shared his testimony with them in the Mayor's Parlour that the Mayor did something very unusual. He accompanied Charles outside his parlour to wave goodbye (normally a Mayor would never leave his parlour on such an occasion). Four days later, the Mayor died suddenly. It is not known if he made a decision for Christ, but he had certainly heard the Gospel.

The Mayor and Mayoress of Carmarthen were so enthralled by Charles Duke's testimony when they heard him speak in the Brangwyn Hall, that they asked all the head children from schools in Carmarthen as well as other civic leaders, to come to the civic reception arranged for Charles. After Charles had graphically related the story of the flight preparation and the walk on the moon, he then told how he had become a Christian. The Mayor, tremendously impressed by what he described as Charles' 'uprightness', told the people that if they could believe the first part of the talk about the preparation, then they could believe the second, about the walk. And if they could believe those two accounts, then they must believe the last part relating to his being born again!

As well as meeting civic leaders, Charles took part in a radio question programme with four sixth-formers from Swansea's Gowerton Comprehensive School, and visited other schools in the area. His visit received a great deal of publicity in the local press, all of it favourable, and he was photographed with groups of school-children which were placed alongside those taken of him in his flight suit back in 1972. Under the headline 'Mission Accomplished for Duke!', the *South Wales Evening Post* gave an excellent report of his meeting in the Brangwyn Hall when about 1,000 came to hear his story. Having spoken at the Swansea, Port Talbot, Llanelli and Carmarthen chapters, his final venue was Bangor University. There he spoke about his visit to South Africa where 150 Zulu chiefs were converted to Christianity after he had talked with them.

It was not just in the South and East of Wales that God was moving in the Fellowship. Up in Llandudno, where they had restarted the chapter nearly four years previously, the Lord worked a miracle in the life of Stephen, son of Mike Russell, who is President of the chapter. While Jean, his wife, was carrying Stephen, Mike was told that he was suffering from cancer and that because of the nature of his illness, the child would be born deformed. When Stephen was born, he was a perfectly healthy baby who has now grown into a 6′2″ young man. Mike was completely healed of the cancer through a combination of the medical profession and much prayer, and he praises God for both.

While there are many advantages to being brought up in a Christian home, one problem which often occurs is that children tend to rely on the experience of their parents without making a complete commitment themselves. This was the case with Stephen and in his teenage years he rebelled against everything his parents stood for. He got himself a motor-bike, grew his hair long, wore the 'right' kind of leathers, and eventually got mixed up with a group of Hells Angels. On one occasion he found himself in a situation that was frightening to say the least, and he suddenly realised that he was on his own. As a result, he sold all his motor-bike gear, bought a car, and came back to where he knew there was support—within the family unit.

When the Llandudno chapter restarted, Stephen began to go along but he was still at the stage of being embarrassed by Christianity. Then one night, Jim Sepulveda was ministering in his quiet, gentle and very 'unAmerican' way, when he stopped and pointed at Stephen and said, 'Young man sitting by the radiator, the Lord wants to deal with you.' Stephen would rather have had a ten-foot hole appear than be singled out in this way, but nevertheless, he went forward for prayer. As Jim prayed over him he began to shake uncontrollably from head to foot and he and his family knew that the Lord had done something tremendous with him.

Since that night, Stephen has taken a Bible correspondence course and is being used by God within the Fellowship, sharing the word of God and giving his testimony. His desire for a deeper Christian experience was made greater following a visit to Greece with Allan Jones. Stephen's eyes were opened to see what God could do as he witnessed miracles of healing and people being set free. When ordinary men and women make themselves available to God, saying, like Isaiah of old, 'Here am I, send me,' then God uses them.

Another chapter in North Wales, in Anglesey was set up in 1982. The man now President, Jim Hodge, a Scotsman, was one of those who attended the first meeting. He had come across the Fellowship while working in North Yorkshire, but not considering himself a businessman, had always refused invitations to go along. This time, when the dinner was announced in his church, he decided to go and see what it was all about, but he had no intention of becoming involved. However, he was so impressed by the love between the men there that he decided to go again.

On the day of the second dinner meeting, Jim learned that the business he worked for had changed hands and the new owners were not sure whether they would get some necessary funding. The speaker that night was David Gomez from California, who had come with Allan

Jones. David was about to pray for a lady when suddenly he stopped and said that there was someone in the meeting who had a business need and if they would go forward, God would meet that need. Jim hesitated but eventually plucked up courage to go to the front where Allan Jones prayed with him. He told Allan that the firm needed £100,000 to keep going. Allan just asked if he would agree with him that God was going to honour his word and Jim nodded his head in affirmation. Within two months all the financial needs of the business had been met.

Jim has been part of the Fellowship on Anglesey since that time, eventually becoming President of the chapter and also a Field Representative. For him, one of the most exciting aspects of the chapter is that they have never had a meeting where there was not at least one person who made a decision for Jesus Christ.

10

The Greatest Miracle is Changed Lives

Allan Jones had visited the North Humberside chapter in 1986. My husband, David, was walking along the street praising God because at that dinner, God had miraculously healed two people of deafness. Suddenly, and with absolute clarity, the Lord spoke to him and said, 'Yes, that is wonderful, but the greatest miracle is changed lives.' And that, of course, is the main thrust of the FGBMFI. Sometimes that may mean someone committing their life to the Lord for the first time, but other times it can mean a Christian having their life totally revolutionised by seeing and experiencing God move in new ways.

The Bible tells us that God loved us so much that he sent his only Son, Jesus, to be the means of our obtaining eternal life (Jn 3:16). Many people today do not go to church and have never heard the message of the Gospel. They do not understand that God is a holy God who cannot look upon sin. Every one of us is sinful (Rom 3:23), and our sin separates us from God. When Jesus died on the cross at Calvary, he took upon himself the sins of the whole world and thus provided a way for us to be reconciled to God. Again, in Romans 10:9–10, we are told that if we confess with our mouth that Jesus is Lord and believe that God raised him from the dead then we will be saved.

There are also many people who have gone to church all their lives but never realised the necessity of making that step of faith and accepting God's gift of eternal life. Sometimes people mistakenly think they can earn their salvation, but Ephesians 2:9–10 are unequivocal: 'For it is by grace you have been saved, through faith—and this is not from yourselves, it is the gift of God—not of works, so that no-one can boast.' Sadly, many people make the initial step yet never seem to grow in their Christian faith. This may be due to lack of teaching or Christian fellowship, but whatever the reason, they need a new awareness of what it means to be a Christian and part of the family of God. The testimonies in this chapter show us the variety of ways God uses to transform people's lives: 'Therefore, if anyone is in Christ, he is a new creation; the old has gone, the new has come' (2 Cor 5:17).

John Walker, a quantity surveyor and now President of the Birmingham chapter, advertised a vacancy in his firm to which only one young man replied. At the beginning of the interview this young man announced, 'The first thing you should know is that I am a Christian.' John was just a 'pew-warmer'; he did not read the Bible or pray, thinking it was a waste of time. He could only reply, 'Well, I go to church.' The young man joined the firm and, considering that John would be a suitable case for 'conversion', kept inviting him to the newly reformed Birmingham chapter. Eventually, after about six months, John went along. His first reaction was that they were crazy—hands in the air, speaking in tongues, even falling down on the floor! Despite this, he felt himself drawn back to those meetings because for the first time in his life he had found sincerity and people who would love him. Two or three months later, at home in the bathroom, he asked Jesus to come into his life.

Before long, John found himself in terrible conflict. He had no doubts about his salvation and was sure God wanted him in the FGBMFI. The problem was, he was a Freemason and involved in three orders: Craft Masonry, Royal Arch and Knights Templar. In the early days after becoming a Christian, no doubts about Freemasonry crossed his mind, but when he was baptised in the Holy Spirit, his difficulties began. Every time he went into a Lodge meeting and participated in the ritual, he felt a profound unease. It was not until he was walking around Gloucester, killing time before a special consecration service of a Knights Templar Preceptory, that he was forced to face up to the problem. Across the road from the Masonic Temple was a Christian bookshop and displayed in the window was a new publication *Can a Christian be a Freemason?* From that moment onwards, every time he went into a bookshop he was confronted with literature questioning the compatibility of Christianity and Freemasonry.

Before the next breakfast meeting, God spoke to John about being obedient. At that time John was the Secretary of the West Midlands Surveyors, his own professional institution. Following a normal committee meeting one evening, he left and got into his car. John always left the radio switched on so that when he turned the ignition it would come on straight away. As he drove down the road John saw his old boss. He stopped the car, wound down the window and they spent some time talking. After wishing him goodnight, John started the car again. Although the engine started first time the radio did not come on—it was completely dead. All the way home John switched the radio on and off, pressing button after button, but nothing happened. He got to within a mile of his home just outside Sutton Coldfield when suddenly an audible voice spoke to him, 'Ask anything in my name and it will be given to you. Command this radio to come on.'

John thought he was going out of his mind so he did nothing. But the same voice came back again, 'Ask anything in my name and it will be given to you. Command this radio to come on.' So he did. And nothing happened. 'Lord,' he said, 'I'm sorry, I'm just hearing things.' The voice came to him again and said, 'Good, you have obeyed me. Now leave the radio switch in the on position because when you stop the car and start it again, the radio will come on.'

Normally when John went out in the evening his wife, Margaret, would leave the garage door open so that he could just turn in off the road straight into the garage. On this particular evening, however, she had not opened the door so John had to stop the car, get out and open it. He got back in the car, switched on the ignition and immediately the radio came on. John rushed into the house and told his wife and family what had happened and then rang Chris, his colleague from the office.

'Chris, do you really think these sort of things happen?' he asked.

'John, of course they happen,' Chris replied. 'I believe that was a test of obedience. The Lord will call upon you to honour that in a much greater way.'

John did not realise just how soon that test of obedience would come. At the breakfast meeting he had the opportunity to share this experience and finished with the words: 'I am just waiting to find out what that test of obedience is.' What he did not know was that the speaker that morning was Ron Price from the Worcester chapter who had stepped in for someone else at short notice. It was the first time he had ever spoken at a meeting and half way through his testimony he stopped and said he believed there were Freemasons in the room.

As he went on to explain how a Christian cannot remain in Freemasonry because there is only one way to God and that is through Jesus Christ, John knew that this was the test of obedience for which God had been preparing him. He went forward to renounce Freemasonry publicly.

That night John had arranged a dinner with two members of his Lodge and he immediately told them that he had renounced Freemasonry. They could not believe what they were hearing but gave him the opportunity to talk at length with them, which he did for two hours. Three weeks later, one of them rang John to say he had decided to be confirmed in the Anglican church and his wife had also rededicated her life to the Lord. Since that time God has used John's testimony to challenge men and be the means of their coming out of Freemasonry into a new relationship with Jesus Christ.

Up in Glasgow, Drew Greenwood, an insurance broker and now a Regional Director, knows all about changed lives. He had come to know the Lord shortly after his father-in-law's death. During the time of refreshment following the funeral service, the minister was asked if the dead man would go to heaven. He had the courage to say he would, but only if he had accepted God's salvation through the death of Jesus Christ on the cross. Challenged by such honesty, Drew and his wife, Marie, came to know the Lord through the help of their local minister. Some time later, Drew began reading about the Holy Spirit and wanted to know more about him. His minister was the obvious person to ask, but although he acknowledged a belief in the power of the Holy Spirit he could not give Drew any help. The following day, however, an elder in the church rang Drew to say his brother-in-law had phoned him from New York and told him about a group of businessmen who believed in the baptism of the Holy Spirit. This man, Jim, then contacted Jim Winter and as a result of the meeting, both he and his wife were baptised in the Holy Spirit.

Drew was taken by Jim to the next FGBMFI dinner where he saw men who had an added dimension to their lives, a freedom and joy which he had not seen before. He joined the chapter some three months later and subsequently received the baptism in the Holy Spirit. It was then he saw God begin to move in his own life and that of his family. His brother John, a company director, highly intellectual and successful, had a son seriously ill in hospital with a chronic heart complaint. There seemed little hope of his recovery and so Drew persuaded John and the hospital that they should allow him to take the young boy to a FGBMFI meeting. After prayer by the members of the chapter, John's son was completely healed.

Feeling a sense of obligation to the Fellowship, John decided to go to the next dinner and put £10 in the offering by way of saying thank you. That night John Hamilton was the speaker. He has an amazing testimony of how God delivered him from alcohol addiction acquired through working as a barman, and he is able to put it across in such a clear and direct way that people cannot fail to respond. John Greenwood may have had everything to make him successful in the world's eyes, but that night he realised he did not have the most important thing—a right relationship with Jesus Christ. He responded to the appeal for salvation and since then, has not only come to know the Lord but has been healed of a malignant tumour in his mouth.

Since his first contact with the Fellowship in 1978, Drew has been greatly used when giving his testimony at various chapters. One evening at the Kilsyth dinner, he felt God prompting him to go over to a man and ask him if anything he had said that evening had struck a chord with him. This man, Jack, said yes, but God couldn't help him because he was an alcoholic, a fighter, as well as abusing his wife and children. Drew told him he had good news, for Paul described himself as the worst of sinners. Still insisting that God could not help him, Jack agreed he would read a book Drew offered to send him. This book was *Prodigal Husband* by Tommy Ashcraft, a truly remarkable story. Shortly afterwards Jack phoned Drew with the question, 'Can something like this really happen?' At the next dinner meeting, in October, Jack came forward to give his life to the Lord.

In February, Drew was again speaking at the Kilsyth chapter when the Lord gave him a word of knowledge that there was a man in the meeting with an ulcer and a blood disorder. When Drew asked that person to come forward to be prayed for, Jack responded but was a little taken aback when Drew cried, 'Praise the Lord!' Having explained that he was praising God because Jack was going to be healed, Drew prayed for him and Jack felt himself falling over under the power of the Holy Spirit. At the March dinner Jack was able to tell Drew that God had healed him.

However, God had still not finished with Jack, for in May he came out once again for prayer. Because of his previous heavy drinking his liver had become diseased, but although he had experienced God's healing power before, Jack did not really think God would be able to do anything this time. Once again, Jack found himself falling on the floor as the power of God touched him and he was completely healed. His wife is overwhelmed because instead of a husband who used to spend all his wages on drink, she now has one who is a tremendous witness to the saving and healing power of the Lord.

Another man, this time in the South-West of England, who has seen both his and his wife's life miraculously changed is David West, now President of the Bath chapter. David suffered from serious depression and his wife was an alcoholic. One day a friend invited him to a dinner at which Ron McCatty was the speaker. As he walked into the room, David was immediately struck by the love and joy of the people, and in spite of his depression he felt at ease, knowing these people had something different. One part of Ron's testimony particularly spoke to David, and that was when he described how he had been clinically dead, for David had also been in that situation following the first of two serious suicide attempts. At the end of his testimony, Ron said there were four people in the room suffering from depression and as David heard him say this, he heard an inner voice saying, 'You're not depressed. What on earth are you taking tranquillisers and sleeping tablets for? You don't need them any more.' David took no sleeping tablets that night, the first time for twelve months, and awoke the next morning after a good sleep, feeling joyful and at peace. He has never had a sleep problem since.

Three months later, the same friend invited David to a breakfast meeting where the speaker was an oil company executive. Halfway through his story, David knew that this was the morning when he would commit his life to Christ. Towards the end of the man's testimony, David began to shake and the blood drained from his face so that his wife leaned over and asked if he was all right. David knew what he had to do, and when the appeal was made a few minutes later, he walked to the front of the meeting and his life was completely changed. Within a few weeks he became a member of the Bath chapter and was baptised in the Holy Spirit.

David's wife, Yvonne, suffering because of loneliness brought about through his workaholicism, had turned to drink as her comfort and, as is often the case, had become addicted. She had sought help from an alcoholic advisory centre in Bristol, but knew that because the addiction was so strong it would be impossible to break.

At that stage, Yvonne was drinking about two pints of Port and a quarter of a bottle of Vodka each evening and probably had only two years at the most to live. At home one evening she heard an audible voice clearly telling her, 'Look at your arms, the alcohol is in your blood.' Yvonne looked around but there was no one in the room. It frightened her so much that she decided to stop drinking. She was then constantly tempted: 'You cannot do without alcohol at Christmas' (and this was early summer). So when she attended a meeting of the Bath chapter of FGBMFI, she asked a member and his wife to pray with her and she was completely set free. A short time after this, Yvonne rededicated her life to the Lord, having made a commitment seven years before.

My husband, David, received a telephone call in November 1982 from a controls engineer called Terry. Terry had been travelling in a colleague's car while on business in Batley and had picked up a *Voice* magazine. When he read the testimonies, Terry realised that these people had something in their lives which he was missing. He rang David to see if there were any meetings in the Hull area and was told there was one the following week and so he booked in. Johnny Hamilton was the speaker, and his testimony was so powerful that Terry was sitting on the edge of his chair. As soon as the appeal was made, he ran out to the front. Shortly afterwards he was baptised in the Holy Spirit.

He went round to see his local vicar, told him what had happened, and got involved at the church. His vicar was not quite sure what to make of him because things began to alter as soon as Terry joined. They had many discussions about the baptism in the Holy Spirit and Terry kept asking him to go to a dinner with him, but without any success. Then one day, a young trainee curate came for a month to help out in the church and one of the first things Rob, the vicar, noticed was that he was wearing an FGBMFI badge. He knew when he was beaten and came along to the next dinner. Rob came forward for prayer that night and the Lord filled him with his Holy Spirit.

Some months after Terry had come to know the Lord, he invited his boss from work to a dinner. Ron came into a new experience with the Lord and so thoroughly enjoyed the atmosphere and the fellowship that he became a member of the chapter, and subsequently trained as a lay reader in the Church of England. Sharing one day about why he had accepted an invitation to come, he explained that he had worked with Terry for some time and knew him well. When Terry became a Christian there was such a transformation in his life that Ron could scarcely believe it, and so when he had the opportunity to 'come and see' for himself, he needed no persuasion.

There are times in every Christian's experience when they find themselves 'off course'. Sometimes this is to such a serious degree that God has to intervene in a miraculous way to bring that person back into a right relationship with himself. Grahame Brown from Keswick, at one time the largest wholesaler of fresh chickens in the country, found himself in such a situation. He had been brought up in a Christian home. Although his parents were thoroughly evangelical, they did not acknowledge baptism in the Holy Spirit. Back in 1965, Graham's parents and brother-in-law were invited by Bill Thompson to the London FGBMFI convention at the Albert Hall. Grahame's brother-in-law later told him that it had been a very exciting meeting, but what had surprised him the most was when the American speaker asked everyone to stand and speak in tongues and Grahame's mother had done just that.

Grahame heard nothing more about the FGBMFI until 1976. (He had come back to God and subsequently been baptised in the Holy Spirit in 1971 while by himself with the Lord.) Then one day Bill Thompson walked into Grahame's office and asked his secretary if he could see him. But because Grahame did not know who Bill was, he did not agree. Bill did not give up. Time and again he went back to the office and asked to see Grahame until he eventually succeeded. Bill introduced himself as knowing Grahame's grandparents from many years previously, and in the course of the conversation, mentioned he had come back to Carlisle to search out people on whom God had laid his hand. He then told Grahame he believed God wanted to use him in the FGBMFI, but Grahame was not interested—he could not stand Americans. Something Bill said however, did get through to Grahame and that was how pleased he was that in the Fellowship he had found a means whereby he and his wife could serve the Lord together. Grahame knew that this was what he wanted too, because he had been trying to serve the Lord alone as there was no opportunity for Florence to minister with him in his church.

When Bill heard that Grahame had booked to go to Hawaii on his own, he said he would give him the names and addresses of the men in the FGBMFI who would welcome him. Grahame had no intention of getting in touch with them, but while he was there he found himself in a church where Yongi Cho was the speaker that week—and all the FGBMFI men were there too. Through his time there God began to prepare Grahame for what he would face in the coming days. In 1979 the serious business problems he had been going through culminated in a court case.

God continued to move in Grahame's life and through Ken Howie from the Scotch Corner chapter, he was invited to the Blackpool convention for the Saturday. He decided to take his son, Simon, with him and they set off at what seemed the unearthly hour of five am for the breakfast meeting. Following the court case, Grahame had become fearful of the world and of meeting people and had lost all his energy for living. He dressed completely in black and went around in constant fear and trepidation. The first thing that struck him as he went into the meeting was that it looked for all the world like a business function but there were no cigarettes or drink and he sensed the same Spirit of God there which had spoken to him back in 1971 when he had been baptised in the Holy Spirit.

The speaker was Jim Fleming from Northern Ireland. At the end of his testimony he invited people who needed the power of the Lord to change them to come forward. Despite all he had gone through, and all the Lord had done in his life, Grahame knew he had habitual sins which he could not conquer by himself. Although he had never gone forward at such a meeting before, that morning he was the first one up on his feet. The chairman of the meeting was Michael Fenton-Jones, chairman of Commercial Union Properties Board, and it was he who came and asked Grahame what he wanted from the Lord. Grahame told him the truth and expected him to back off a little, but Michael did not flinch, he simply put his hands on Grahame's head and spoke in tongues.

Grahame finds it hard to express how he felt at that moment. Not only was a tremendous weight lifted off him, but he felt as if he was moving from total darkness into light. His tears were shared not only by his son, Simon, but also by Bill Thompson. Although he had not seen Grahame since that day in 1976, Bill had never stopped praying for him and he knew that that morning God was bringing into being the word he had given to Grahame in 1976 that he had a work for him in the FGBMFI. Since then God has taken Grahame through yet more wonderful experiences and he has shared his testimony at almost 200 chapters throughout the United Kingdom, Ireland and the West coast of America.

John Wright, part of whose testimony has already been mentioned, learned that even as a Christian and having a leading role in the Fellowship, it was necessary for God to intervene and bring about changes in his life. By 1982 he was owner of a film company and chairman of a film bank, and despite some uncertainty in preceding years, he was confident of the future in terms of finance and health. He regularly gave his testimony in FGBMFI chapters, boasting in the faithfulness of the Lord and seeing a never-ending vista of the Lord's blessing as a reward for his obedience. At this stage, God stepped in to do what the Apostle John describes in chapter 15 of his gospel as the work of a gardener who prunes the branches of the vine in order that they may become more fruitful. Later, in the book of Revelation, the same writer records God's message to the church at Laodicea, part of which was: 'Those whom I love I rebuke and discipline.' So it was that God began to use the circumstances of John's life in order to remind him that everything we have and are is to be found in Jesus.

As the first quarter of 1982 drew to a close, the film bank (United Media Finance) was establishing its policies and beginning to invest substantial amounts in television drama, but the film company (UMP) was finding it more and more difficult to increase orders to pay for spiralling costs. John found he had to work away from home all week in London, putting a strain on family life, and as the workload increased so his work with FGBMFI began to fall away—there just wasn't time.

In the second quarter, problems with union blacking of one of their best customers and a delay in starting a new contract meant more money had to be pumped into UMP. At this stage John was not too worried, thinking it would just take a little longer than expected for the company to become profitable. Before long, however, more trouble appeared—this time from a most unexpected quarter. Having always experienced good health, in fact, almost taking it for granted, John went as usual for his annual medical check-up in April. His doctor advised the removal of a mole on his arm which was duly carried out by a Harley Street specialist—a small operation carried out under local anaesthetic.

A week later, John received a disturbing telephone call from his doctor. The mole had turned out to be malignant. Not fully understanding the implications, John asked what he meant. 'Well—to put it bluntly,' said the doctor, 'your life is no longer insurable. You have cancer.' John's father had died of cancer at the age of fifty-six, and John always thought he would be terrified if he was ever diagnosed as having the disease but he was amazed to find himself at peace. He was told that urgent arrangements had been made for the area surrounding the mole to be removed by surgery and replaced by a skin graft.

Having experienced the healing power of God, John was in no doubt that God could heal him but he had to decide whether to go ahead with the operation or leave the situation in God's hands. Right up to the evening prior to the operation when he entered University College Hospital and asked the chaplain to pray with him, John was still undecided. He read the Bible, praying for guidance, wanting only to do God's will, but no word came to him and eventually he telephoned a Christian doctor, asking God to speak through the advice given. His friend recommended that he have the operation and trust God for the outcome. Ten days later, when the bandages were removed, the skin grafts had taken a hundred percent and John worshipped God for his goodness.

Within one week of this operation, John's solicitor had told him that a case for breach of contract was to be brought against him in the High Court in two weeks' time. Thinking it too ridiculous for words, John had no worries. It was, in fact, a rather sad case. A man who had lived with the family for two years on and off had asked John to back the development of an idea. Eventually, after the advice of two sets of design engineers to the effect that the idea was impracticable, John withdrew and returned the patents application and work done to his friend. Two years later a similar device was marketed but was a complete failure. The complaint against John was that had he continued to invest money his friend would have succeeded.

Once again, John found himself in a dilemma. A verse in the Bible tells us to 'settle on your way to court, lest you be cast into prison.' However, the £50,000 claimed was not only a ridiculous figure but one John could not have paid even had he wanted to. Searching the Scriptures he came across the verse in Psalm 37 which says: 'The wicked lie in wait for the righteous, seeking their lives, but the Lord will not leave them in their power, or let them be condemned when brought to trial.'

The case was to be heard in London, a long way from Norwich, so John hoped he would escape the attention of the local press but he was quickly disillusioned. A reporter from their local paper had been specially briefed to report the proceedings and what newspaper could resist the opening line of the plaintiff: 'My Lord, John Wright is a confidence trickster'. For two long hot weeks in June, John sat and listened gloomily knowing that the costs (eventually over £11,000) could not be claimed even if he won because the plaintiff was legally aided.

In his summing up, the judge went through all the circumstances of the case, nothing in his face or manner indicating the outcome. After sitting for what seemed an age, John heard him say, 'The allegations against the defendant are in my view outrageous and totally unsupported by any of the evidence presented . . .' Overwhelmed by God's goodness, John was sitting and giving praise for his deliverance when from the judge came a most unexpected comment: 'Mr Wright is a credit to his faith.' Suddenly the pressure and desperation he had felt as a Christian being publicly named a confidence trickster came to the surface and he broke down and cried.

In the space of just a few months, John had experienced a severe buffeting. As many other Christians in similar situations have done, he asked the question, 'Why is all this happening to me?' He had prayed against the cancer, against the case coming to court, for the business to prosper, in every one being confident of the outcome. After all, he knew God's promises: 'I am the Lord that healeth thee.' 'No weapon forged against my servant will prosper.' 'I will prosper the work of your hands.'

Although the Lord finally answered his prayers for help, he had to go through a confusing and difficult time first. John had searched his heart to find if there was some great sin he needed to repent of or whether there was a lesson he was too blind to learn. Then God spoke to him in his situation: 'You must let me carry you.' To John, the Lord was just like a father offering to lift a very self-confident and independent three-year-old over some rough ground. The following week God confirmed what he was trying to say when John heard for the first time the lovely story of 'Footprints'.

> There was a man who had a dream. In this dream he was walking along the beach with Jesus. As he looked back he saw two sets of footprints going back through his life, but in certain places—when the going had been really tough—there was only one set of footprints. 'Lord,' he said, 'Why

did you leave me when it was tough?' Jesus turned to him and smiled, 'That's when I carried you.'

Lying in bed, seeking further understanding, John had a vivid mental picture of a huge forty-foot wave bearing down on him as he swam in the sea. In front of him was some driftwood as if from a shipwreck. 'Take hold of the wood,' the Lord said, 'stop swimming.' As John obeyed he realised that the wood was the cross and as he clung on, it lifted him over three great waves which then passed harmlessly beneath him. As they did so the Lord spoke again, 'I am your buoyancy. Look behind you.' John looked back to see the three waves hit the beach and subside into froth and bubbles. Once again the Lord spoke to him, 'Everything that comes against you is an impostor.' Then John realised God was showing him that as we cling to the cross, God carries us over whatever seems about to engulf us.

For John, the business and financial problems did not go away. Indeed, eventually he had to call in a receiver to the film company and subsequently lost his seat as chairman of the finance company. What he had learned, and continued to learn in the coming months, was that God was his rock, his fortress, his deliverer and that 'in Him I will trust'.

In his letter to the Philippians, chapter 3, the Apostle Paul emphasises that despite the tremendous revelations given to him by the Lord, he had still not 'arrived' in the spiritual sense, but he was pressing on towards the goal set by God. Whatever the Lord has done in our lives there is always still more to be changed, whether we are new or longstanding Christians. We should be encouraged by the words of Paul to the Christians at Philippi when he tells them to forget what is past—whatever the failures or disappointments—and keep going on:

No, dear brothers, I am still not all I should be but I am bringing all my energies to bear on this one thing: forgetting the past and looking forward to what lies ahead, I strain to reach the end of the race and receive the prize for which God is calling us up to heaven because of what Christ Jesus did for us' (Phil 3:13–14, The Living Bible).

11

There Is Healing—in the Name of Jesus

On the last occasion when Jesus was with his disciples on earth he gave them the great commission to go into all the world and preach the Gospel to every creature. This is the vision of the FGBMFI, and its fulfilment is its number one priority. But there is more. Jesus also said of those who would believe that 'In my name . . . they shall speak with new tongues . . . they shall lay hands on the sick, and they shall recover' (Mk 16:17–19).

Healing is a controversial issue in many churches and among many Christians, and while it is true that some people do not receive healing, God's word is unequivocal. We read in John's gospel how Jesus told the disciples: 'I tell you the truth, anyone who has faith in me will do what I have been doing. He will do even greater things than these, because I am going to the Father. And I will do whatever you ask in my name, so that the Son may bring glory to the Father. You may ask me for anything in my name, and I will do it' (Jn 14:12–14).

The Fellowship has always preached a 'full gospel' and in this chapter we will hear the stories of just a few who have experienced healing in the name of Jesus. We will also see how God is sovereign in all things: he decides the time and the method. It is also important to stress that healing is more than physical. People need to be healed from hurts, bitterness and resentment because these can be the cause of physical ailments as well as emotional problems.

One of the most amazing testimonies comes from Llanelli in South Wales. Roy Peacock, the visiting speaker, had been working hard all day and then drove to the chapter meeting, arriving about 7.15 pm which meant he had no time even for a wash and brush-up. The ministry time at the end of the meeting was quite lengthy. Feeling extremely tired, Roy looked at his watch as the last person came forward for prayer. It was 10.45 pm. He felt very lacking in faith and not too enthusiastic about praying for anyone else. However, he listened carefully as the lady told her story. She had come for prayer on behalf of her mother who was eighty-one and had been in a wheel-chair for the last eighteen years. A severe arthritic condition had destroyed the mobility of her legs and moved through her spine and she was unable to take more than three steps without falling over. She was in such pain that she continuously used pain-killers of the morphine group. Her daughter was a medical sister and therefore in a position to give Roy a full professional assessment of her mother's condition. It was so complex and Roy was so tired that he could not absorb the enormity of the problem and he simply prayed that the Lord would touch this old lady.

For the next two days Roy was involved with meetings in central Wales and then he returned to Gorseinon in the South. He was speaking in a church and the pastor asked Roy if a Mrs Thompson could say a few words. As Mrs Thompson passed Roy on her way to the front, she smiled at him. Roy could not place her, but as she spoke he realised it was the lady from the Llanelli dinner who had come out for prayer at 10.45 pm three nights before.

Mrs Thompson told the congregation how when she got home from the dinner, she let herself into the house and found her mother on the floor. Thinking her mother had died, she let out a scream but then the old lady stirred and so her daughter lifted her into bed. She said she had watched the news on the television and a little later was using the remote control to find another programme. Suddenly she began to feel strange and glancing up at the clock noticed it was 10.45 pm and that was all she remembered until that moment. Next morning, shortly before 8 am, Mrs Thompson heard footsteps in the hall and went to the door to see who was passing through. She discovered that her mother, who had not walked for eighteen years, was walking from her bedroom into the kitchen to make the breakfast. She finished this remarkable story by affirming that the healing was from the Lord.

Some of the congregation stared at her in amazement, a few of them in evident disbelief. Noticing this, Mrs Thompson wagged her finger at them and said authoritatively, 'And what is more, to prove to you that God has healed my mother, I have brought her here tonight.' Pointing to the back of the church she said, 'There she is!' Everybody turned to see a little old lady sitting in a wheel-chair. Someone took away the foot-rest and, to the astonishment of the church, this lady slowly stood up, raised her arms (which were full of old fractures) to heaven, and walked the length of the building on legs that medically speaking could not work. Her face was radiant and as she reached the front, somewhat to Roy's embarrassment, she threw her arms around him and kissed him. For the rest of that series of meetings there was not one spare seat in the church!

Rodney and Judy Radcliffe had moved to a house in Dulwich in 1985. As the house needed painting, they prayed about it and asked a local man called Mr

McKeown to do the job. Two weeks after he had completed the work, he came to tell them he had cancer and the doctor believed it was terminal. More in obedience than faith, Rodney prayed for him and when he went back into hospital the second biopsy showed no trace of cancer. It was not until a year later, at the Blackheath chapter, that this man came to know the Lord. Then in early November 1986 he phoned Rodney saying, 'Rodney, I am desperate. My son-in-law, Paul, has fallen off a roof and has multiple face lacerations, broken legs, ankles, ribs and pelvis. Will you pray for him?'

That evening Rodney was visiting a man who had been due to go into hospital to have a pin put through a cartilage but he had been healed at the previous dinner of the Blackheath chapter. Their faith lifted by what the Lord had done, they began to pray for Paul until twelve o'clock that night. At 2 am Paul went into the operating theatre. The next morning, all they could find wrong with him was a broken leg! Not only was he healed physically but the Lord took away all the shock and bitterness, because there had been insufficient safety precautions taken by the company. As a result of this, Mr McKeown says that whereas before he had believed in God, he now really knows him.

Coming out of the Norwich dinner meeting about midnight, Alan Pimlott was met by three ladies who had been there, one of whom asked if he would pray for her and her friends. He noticed that she had been crying and then she told him after five years of tests the doctors had finally told her it would be impossible for her to have a child. What she had heard in the meeting that night, however, had given her faith but not enough courage to go forward to be prayed for. After Alan had prayed that a miracle would take place, another of the ladies asked if he would also pray for her. She used a stick because of arthritis in the knee, so Alan knelt down and prayed for healing in the name of Jesus.

Four months later, Alan and his wife, Anne, were invited to lead the worship at the first Cambridge dinner. They got lost on the way there and so by the time they arrived everything was underway and they slipped into two seats at the back of the room. The lady sitting next to Alan smiled at him and said, 'You don't remember me, do you?' Alan apologised and said he didn't. 'Do you remember about four months ago you prayed for three ladies? I had not been able to move my leg but when I got up the next morning, it was completely healed.' As she finished telling him that, the lady who had not been able to have children walked in—four months' pregnant!

When Alan was speaking at the Nottingham chapter, a lady came forward for prayer because her left hand was totally useless. As a child of seven she had been told not to touch the milk bottles but she did and at the same time tripped and fell, severing all the tendons in that hand. Alan prayed for her healing but also came against the root cause of the problem. This took her right back to the time of the accident and enabled healing of the memories to take place. The next morning when she woke up she had regained the complete use of her hand and wrote a sixteen-page letter to Alan. It was fifty-three years since she had damaged the hand, but God had worked a miracle.

Sometimes the Lord seems to use people in particular ministries, and Alan has certainly been used a great deal in helping people with arthritic problems. In Cornwall a lady came and asked if Alan would pray for her leg which was in a leg-iron. When he first looked down, Alan was scared stiff. But rebuking this he got down on the floor, removed the iron, and took her foot in his hand. Alan prayed against the problem in the name of Jesus and then told the lady to move her toes. She screamed out in disbelief as she saw them move. He then told her to move her ankle and as she stood up her leg was healed and she waved her leg-iron in the air. She then told them that she was staying with her son and daughter-in-law who were atheists. 'What can they say when I walk in healed?' she wondered.

One evening, Alan was invited to speak at the New Town chapter in Wales. A lady and her husband who were on holiday from Leicester were invited to the dinner. The man was not a Christian but his wife had prayed for him for thirty years. The morning of the dinner she was out walking and told the Lord she could not take any more, she would have to leave her husband. When they were asked to the dinner she fully expected her husband to refuse, but much to her surprise he accepted. When Alan made the appeal for salvation, his was the first hand to go up. His wife was almost beside herself, but then the Lord showed Alan, through a word of knowledge, that a couple there had serious marriage problems. So they both came out together and Alan was able to pray for them. One of the men in their party had gone away from the Lord and he made a rededication of his life. These two men are now officers in the Leicester chapter.

The Lord has gentle ways of rebuking us, just as he did the disciples when they wanted to send away the children whose parents brought them to Jesus for healing. The Bible tells us that Jesus was indignant and said, 'Let the little children come to me, and do not hinder them, for the kingdom of God belongs to such as these' (Mk 10:14). Jim Faulds was convening a dinner meeting in the Lorne Hotel when a man came in with a group of children. Jim was rather annoyed because he thought the meeting was unsuitable for them, especially when one of the little girls began to cry. She was only about ten and Jim thought she was crying because she was bored, but when it came to the time of ministry this little girl came up to him. Asking what she wanted prayer for, she told him her ears were very sore and painful and that was why she had been crying. The doctor had given her some drops but they had not helped. Jim put his hands on her ears, prayed, and took them away. She said they felt no different so he prayed again and the next time he took his hands away her face lit up with joy because all the pain had gone. Her father later told Jim that she had become a real evangelist in her school.

At the 1983 Blackpool convention, Don Latham was sitting in the Friday afternoon meeting listening to Kenneth Copeland preaching on faith. Don was to be the speaker at the evening dinner and all he could think was 'how can I follow this man?' Then the Lord told Don that he would prepare him. At the end of the afternoon session some friends from Warminster came and told him they had taken a lady out because she was in such pain and would Don go with them to pray for her. Driving along the sea-front, Don asked God what he should say to Jean and all he could hear was 'I want her to know Jesus.'

Jean took some time to answer the door because she felt so ill, but eventually they went in and Don sat beside her on the settee. He said, 'Jean, all that God has been saying to me is that he wants you to know Jesus.' She told him she would love that but had so many fears and doubts, to which Don replied, 'God will deal with them.' He then put his hand on her shoulder and said, 'Jean, I set you free in Jesus' name.' She gasped and fell back on the settee and started to say, 'Jesus,' just as if he was standing in front of her. One of the men who was standing in the room fell on his face to the floor, the power of God was so strong. Jean then started squeezing Don's hands so hard that he wondered what was wrong, but she told him she had been unable to do anything with her hands before because there was no feeling in them. That night she came to the convention and before Don spoke he asked her to tell the people what had happened that afternoon. Such was the faith generated that when Don finished speaking, fifty people came forward for salvation. First her daughter, then her husband, a confirmed atheist, came to know the Lord and two weeks later he was baptised in the Holy Spirit.

On another occasion Don was speaking at a London convention with Ian Andrews. He had written to a number of people he knew in the area to invite them along, but only one lady he had met in Jerusalem replied. She could only come to the afternoon session when Ian Andrews was to be the speaker. Don met her in the hotel foyer and they went upstairs to the meeting. This was difficult because her knees were heavily bandaged and she told Don her body was full of arthritis. As they were sitting in the meeting, Don had a vision of her running down the stairs and at that moment she turned to him with tears in her eyes and said, 'I have been healed.' He told her to go and take the bandages off and she came back so excited because she could actually bend.

When the afternoon session was over, they walked out together and Don noticed that she was still hobbling and looked out of balance. He sat her on a chair and held out her legs—one was much shorter than the other. In the name of Jesus he commanded her short leg to grow, and as it did the thought crossed his mind, 'Lord, do you know how to stop?' But her legs came into perfect balance and the vision Don had of her running down the stairs came to pass that day. Having a prior engagement to attend her church social, she had to leave. But at midnight she wrote a letter to Don saying how wonderful it was to be free of pain.

Early in 1987 the Westminster chapter was reformed, aimed at reaching MPs and top businessmen. The first meeting was held in the Café Royal with about 120 people there and Don as the main speaker. Nigel Found, a stockbroker, gave a lovely testimony and his two teenage children were among those who came forward when Don gave the appeal. Not only did they give their hearts to the Lord, but they were also baptised in the Holy Spirit. Don encouraged them to pray for their father who had come out for healing and as they prayed with him, he fell down under the power of the Holy Spirit and got up healed. What a wonderful confirmation of the fact that what God wants is people who are prepared to let him work through them.

Many people came forward for salvation, among them ten men, while many others came for healing. Don told the people that God had given him words of knowledge about many present who needed healing and he mentioned the specific needs before closing the meeting with prayer. He then encouraged people to come forward and many were praying with their guests. A girl started to scream and thinking it could be something to do with the occult, Don went over to investigate. She was weeping hysterically and when he asked her what was wrong, she told him that she had been blind but could now see. She was Jewish, and the lady who brought her to the dinner was the nurse who had delivered her baby. Don went over to the microphone and said, 'Before you leave this meeting, I think I should share the good news with you. A girl came here tonight totally blind in one eye but the Lord has healed her.' Every member of the FGBMFI in the room was needed to pray for the flood of people who responded when they saw what God had done.

The *Athlone Observer*, 5th June 1986, carried an article entitled 'Miracles Do Happen' together with a large photograph of a lady getting up out of a wheel-chair. This account began:

> It's not every day that one is afforded the opportunity of seeing a miracle happen before one's eyes. Last week at a

function in Portlaoise, this writer witnessed such an event. The occasion in question was a dinner hosted by the Full Gospel Business Men's Fellowship International—an almost world-wide ministry of people coming together in the name of Jesus.

Allan Jones had been invited over to the South of Ireland to speak at a number of chapters and it was after he had shared his testimony that this miracle occurred. Margaret McGree, the lady of the story, had been confined to a wheel-chair after breaking her spine in an accident which left her crippled. She was living in a purpose-built maisonette which had all essential conveniences, including an outer ramp for easy access to her home.

Speaking to the astonished group of dinner guests, Margaret said that during the meal she had a progressive burning sensation in her legs which had been numb since the accident two years ago. She was able to stand up and walk a few paces without any discomfort or feeling of weakness in her legs. Concluding the article, the writer explained that Allan was an Englishman who had 'successfully' prayed for people with various illnesses, and he was in the country on behalf of the FGBMFI 'whose aim is to bring people to Jesus through a link with a loving community.'

There is a sequel to this story. The photograph showed Allan holding Margaret's hand and there was also a man at the other side of her. He came from Limerick and went home to tell his sister of this miracle. She was so touched by it that she went along to the next dinner meeting and gave her heart to the Lord.

At one of the Bristol chapter breakfasts there was a lady called Rose, sixty-nine years of age, who had never been able to walk unaided. She could not lift her legs and moved around by shuffling a zimmer frame on wheels. Ron McCatty was leading the meeting and during the ministry time someone brought her over to him. As he took hold of her hands she said, 'I do not have any faith.' Ron thought to himself that this was not a very good start but nevertheless asked if she thought God could heal her. 'If God can do anything for me,' she said, 'you should know, but I must tell you I do not have any faith.' Normally a quiet, gentle man, Ron became slightly indignant and said, 'Be healed in Jesus' name anyway!' With that she fell flat on her back and all the people in the room fell silent. They waited and waited. Twenty minutes went by and all sorts of thoughts flashed through Ron's mind. He could see the newspaper headline: 'Minister Struck Woman and She Fell Dead!'

After what seemed like an eternity, she eventually opened her eyes and rolled onto her hands and knees, something she had never done before. 'Look, I'm moving,' she said, and then got onto her knees, took hold of Ron's hand and shouted, 'Look, I am standing!' Ron heard himself saying, 'You will do more than that—walk!' With everyone's eyes on her she began walking round the room and the people erupted into praise. She was even able to walk down the steep stairs of the hotel and was so full of joy she came back the next month to tell everyone what Jesus had done for her.

In the book of Acts we read how people became Christians after seeing the Apostles perform miracles in the name of Jesus, and God still uses this method to bring some people to himself. Paul Jinadu, a converted Muslim, came to know the Lord after seeing God perform a miracle of healing. When he gave his testimony at the Southampton chapter, a Muslim lady came and said she too would believe if God would show her a miracle. One of the friends who had come with her had a deformed thumb which she could not move, so Paul told her to look at this lady's hand. He prayed and within a few seconds she was able to straighten her thumb. Not only did the Muslim lady come to know the Lord but others were set free from bondages or had demons cast out of them, all in the name of Jesus.

It is wonderful to see and experience the miracle of instant healing, but this is not the only way the Lord works. James tells us that every good and perfect gift comes from God and there are times when he uses the skills of doctors to effect our healing. There are times too, when despite much prayer, and sometimes fasting, healing does not take place.

In his book *God Wants You Whole* Selwyn Hughes describes what a struggle it was to write as his wife was suffering an illness from which she later died. He says that one conviction, reinforced day after day by the Holy Spirit, kept him going: 'God's word is true, no matter how circumstances or situations argue against it.' He goes on to explain that he does not know all the reasons why some are healed and others are not but the following statement he makes in the Preface sums up the dilemma: '"The subject of healing," said a preacher, "is one of the greatest mysteries in the universe. We are big enough to ask the questions, but not big enough to understand the answers."'

12

Their Voice Has Gone out into All the Earth

'If the full Gospel Business Men's Fellowship International has to go around the world, then it has to have a Voice.' So said Thomas Nickel to Demos Shakarian on that never-to-be-forgotten Saturday morning in 1952 in Clifton's Cafeteria. The American *Voice* magazine was used in the United Kingdom and Ireland but in 1978 it was decided that a European edition was called for, though quite a number of the American *Voice* continue to be circulated. The Brussels office took responsibility for publishing the magazine which is now printed in fifteen European languages.

Christians sometimes criticise *Voice* magazine because it does not appear to be 'religious'. That, of course, is the whole point. It is aimed at the non-Christian and is therefore designed to attract those who would not normally pick up Christian literature. *Voice* is a powerful tool for evangelism and the magazines are given away free at outreach meetings as well as through doctors' and dentists' waiting-rooms, hospitals, supermarkets, hotels, country shows—in fact, wherever openings are found by the local chapters. The financial commitment of individual members and chapters to *Voice* is considerable, but

God has wonderfully blessed this ministry. As with the outreach meetings of the Fellowship, *Voice* is made up of testimonies of ordinary working men telling how God has changed their lives and more often than not, the lives of their families. Stories come from all over Europe and occasionally ones from the American, Asian, African or Australian *Voice* editions are included, helping to remind us that the Fellowship is truly international.

The following incident tells us something about the powerful effect of *Voice* magazine. Beryl Jones, from South Wales, placed *Voice* magazines in the University of Swansea library. While doing so one day, she was introduced to a Mexican lady studying for a Ph.D at the university, and also a lady from Ethiopia. She gave each one a magazine and they were so excited that they asked if she could give them a few to send to their husbands. Beryl invited the ladies to her home and showed them a video from the 1983 Blackpool convention. While they were watching, one lady fell over under the power of the Spirit and both received the baptism in the Holy Spirit.

A little while later, Beryl was coming out of the library when she met the Ethiopian lady who said her husband had come over and wanted to know more about the FGBMFI. That night Allan Jones was to be at Phil and Beryl's house, so she invited the couple to come for the evening. It turned out to be the only evening her husband could come. This man had a remarkable experience and was interested in having further copies of *Voice* but in French because he was working in Niger which is French speaking. He was Chief Administrator of the United Nations Economic Commission in that country, and that week he was returning with his wife who had finished her course. As far as they knew, they would not be returning to Britain again. God's timing is always perfect, but he requires our obedience to the promptings of the Holy Spirit.

Up in North Wales, in Llandudno, people have also seen how God can use *Voice* magazine. Five hundred copies were placed in hotels, hospitals, police stations and other public places. One young man, who worked in the Cheshire Homes in Colwyn Bay, had been into everything trying to find a solution to his problems and he was desperate. He went into the local library and picked up a copy of *Voice*. When he read it he knew this was what he had been searching for. He went along to a dinner and gave his heart to the Lord. A lady in Llandudno picked up a copy of *Voice* in a shop and rang the President, Mike Russell to ask for help because her husband was an alcoholic. In the same week a young man read one while in the washeteria and rang Mike up. The officers of the chapter were able to meet and help both these people.

A church in East Kilbride had been searching for good Christian literature to give out and after looking at everything available, had decided that *Voice* was the best by a long way. The chapter offered them 100 copies a month and sent the first batch in December. In February eleven people from East Kilbride came to the dinner and four came to know the Lord, three of them young men in their early twenties. Another lady who had read a *Voice* magazine then read *The Happiest People on Earth*. She phoned Drew Greenwood to ask about the chapter and he invited her to the next meeting. A few days later she phoned again to ask if she could bring some guests along. She brought seven people with her and after hearing Paul Jinadu share his testimony, four of them came to know the Lord.

The Birmingham chapter has also seen results from their use of *Voice* and now place 100 copies of each issue of the French and German editions in the National Exhibition Centre where many people, particularly Europeans, regularly visit. One day a man phoned the chapter President, John Walker, and said, 'You don't know me, my name is Terry. . . . I was preaching in a particular Assembly on Sunday against the gifts of the Holy Spirit. When I had finished a man came up to me and said I had not done it with much conviction and gave me a copy of *Voice* magazine. Once I started reading, I could not put it down.' The chapter dinner had just been held, so he came to a prayer meeting where there were only about five men. This man had a remarkable story. He was the eldest of seven children and his father had terminal cancer. The family decided that as the eldest he should be the one to break the news to their father. Eventually, he told him and his father said, 'Don't worry, I am going to be with Jesus.' His son had once made a commitment to Christ, but had since lapsed. His father's words had such an impact on him that he rededicated his life to the Lord.

As the group got down to prayer, Terry began to speak in tongues immediately. No one had said anything to him about speaking in tongues and he was almost beside himself with excitement. He then asked if they believed in healing, as his wife was ill. Following the example of Paul in Acts 19:12, the men prayed over a handkerchief for Terry to take home to his wife. He arrived home past midnight, threw the bedroom door open, and began speaking in tongues. Terry told his wife what had happened and asked her to lie on the handkerchief. In the morning she was completely healed.

David Rose of the Ipswich chapter, who is involved in farming and land drainage, got up early one morning to pray about a problem. As soon as he started to pray God gave him a vision. He was with a group of people from the Fellowship at the Royal Show and they were handing out *Voice* magazines. But then he saw that it was not an ordinary copy but a special one concerned with farming. David's mind began to tick over. He thought that it would be good to have someone who grew apples, someone who worked on a farm, and another who lectured in an agricultural institution to write their testimonies for a special edition. He was so excited that he wanted to share the idea with someone, but as it was still rather early he waited until a more respectable time before phoning Dillon Harris as he lived close to the Royal Showground. Dillon told him that he had wanted to do something like this a few years previously but there didn't seem to be the people in the Fellowship at that time to carry out such an undertaking.

David phoned Blair Scott, the Editor of *Voice*, and they talked about the idea. Blair agreed in principle and offered his help. David had never written anything in his life and didn't know how to go about it, so he kept putting off getting something together. The task seemed too enormous for him on his own, so he asked God to provide someone to help him. David had been invited to speak at the Nottingham chapter and he spoke about this vision. Afterwards an agricultural journalist, Alan Barnsdale, offered to help in any way he could. When David asked Alan how he wrote his stories, Alan said that he wrote them out, corrected them until he could not read them and then wrote them out again. The fact that a professional journalist found it difficult gave David considerable hope, but he still failed to do anything about it.

Some time later David was up in court for driving without due care and attention to which he pleaded guilty but explained mitigating circumstances to the bench. All three magistrates sat and doodled, and about half way through his plea, David realised that he might as well sit down because they had already decided on the fine. Not long after this he had a dream in which he was standing at the bench again, but this time it was Judgement Day and God was presiding. He saw himself trying to explain mitigating circumstances as to why he had done nothing about writing a Farmers' *Voice* magazine. As a result of this dream, David realised that he had been given a commission and it was up to him to carry it out to the best of his ability, not necessarily perfectly.

David immediately took a week off work and visited people whose names had been given to him in various aspects of farming. He spent the next six weeks getting the stories together, crossing them out until he couldn't read them, and then getting his wife, Anita, to type them again and again. Thirty thousand copies of this special edition were published in the first year and used in various shows around the country. The Bath chapter gave out over 8,000 at the Bath and West Show. The Isle of Wight chapter posted a copy to every farmer on the island. In 1986 a further 40,000 copies were published. Finance for the first edition was raised by asking ten people to give £400 each. The second edition was financed by offering them to the chapters for ten pence each and with the extra money from the tax benefits of covenanting, the costs were covered. The project was not easy to organise, but the Fellowship had a special fund to underwrite the exercise and God blessed the venture. At various shows around the country over 100 men and women have given their lives to Jesus on the show stands as a result of this magazine.

Early in 1987, over 400 officers of the FGBMFI met for a weekend in Blackpool to seek God and receive from him a new impetus for the work to which they had been called. Many of these men gave their testimonies, including Tim Bishopp. He described how, two years ago, he had been in a presidents' meeting at Stoke-on-Trent when David Rose had spoken about the Farmers' *Voice* magazine and the Lord gave him a vision of the Ardingly Show in East Sussex. They arranged to have a large tent at the 1986 summer show where they would give away free cups of tea and coffee and at the same time copies of Farmers' *Voice*.

The weather forecast for the show that year was terrible, but believing the word of God in John 14 where Jesus says, 'If you ask anything in my name, I will do it,' they came together and prayed for three days of good weather so that thousands of people would come. On the morning of the first day it was pouring with rain. Some of the Christians were saying, 'Oh well, praise God for the rain,' which made Tim very angry because he knew it was not the right answer to prayer. So they prayed for the rain to stop, which it did immediately, and the show had three days of the best weather ever.

On that first day, they did not have much success and they realised that they were trying to do this work in their own strength. Although one person came to know the Lord, this was not fulfilling the vision Tim had received. So for the second and third days they prayed for a real anointing of the Holy Spirit. The Lord pointed them to Matthew chapter 8 where the leper meets Jesus coming down the mountainside and says, 'Lord, if you are willing, you can make me clean.' Reaching out his hand to touch him, Jesus says, 'I am willing. Be clean.' The scripture tells us that he was immediately cured of his leprosy.

Later on the second day, an old lady came into the tent crippled with arthritis. Tim felt it was right to tell her the story of the leper and she was instantly healed. In the last two days fifty-seven people people came to know Jesus, countless others were baptised in the Holy Spirit, and many were healed. They gave away 4,000 drinks, and every person who received one was told about Christ. 6,000 copies of Farmers' *Voice* were also given away, as well as many copies of *The Happiest People on Earth*. Prince Charles, who had opened the show, passed close to the FGBMFI tent and readily accepted two

Voice magazines and a copy of Demos' book, and at the next men's meeting they prayed for him and the entire Royal Family.

At the election meeting of the Bath chapter it was announced that no one was looking after the *Voice* magazine ministry, so they prayed that someone would be led by the Holy Spirit to take this up. They didn't make any decision then, but left it that if the Lord spoke to anyone they would contact the officers. That night David West realised that God had saved his job as a sales representative when he had been depressed, and he saw no reason why he should not be a sales representative for Jesus with the *Voice* magazine. He tackled the whole *Voice* ministry as a selling job, setting up about fifty locations in a variety of areas: fish-and-chip shops, stores and surgeries, as well as many churches. They now circulate over 2,000 of every edition and send 100 copies each time to Ghana.

Although God has used this distribution, it is in the area of personal witnessing that David has found the magazine so useful. His job as a sales representative gives him plenty of opportunities and he gives one to every customer he meets. Both of his ex-sales directors and their wives had become Christians, one of the couples being led to the Lord in their lounge at home. Sadly, the wife of one director died in August 1986, but they had the assurance she had gone to be with Jesus.

David had the opportunity of sharing how the Lord had healed him of depression with the lady purchasing manager of an engineering company, a very hard-headed business woman who even frightened the managing director! David gave her copies of *Voice* magazine over a period of time. One day she told him how worried she was because she had to undergo surgery for a tumour in her breast. Having read in the magazines that Jesus still heals today, she asked if she could attend an FGBMFI meeting. An open meeting was to be held three days later when Ian Andrews was to be the guest speaker. That night she went forward for prayer and much to her surprise, found herself on the floor by the power of the Holy Spirit. Getting to her feet she discovered the tumour had disappeared and a few months later, David led her in a prayer of commitment to Christ in her home.

On another occasion, David was talking about divine healing with a lady buyer in a South Wales paper mill. She said she could not believe it so David left her a *Voice* magazine to read. When he made his return visit, he did not see her at first and so gave her boss a magazine. Just before David left, this lady came into the office and told both men that a few days after receiving that *Voice* magazine, she had gone to church for the first time in many years, heard the Gospel, and accepted Jesus as her Saviour.

A man picked up a *Voice* magazine in a local church and phoned David to ask about the Fellowship. He was invited to a breakfast meeting and was saved, baptised in the Holy Spirit, and set free from addiction to smoking and alcohol. He had been a very heavy drinker, to the point where it was causing problems in his relationship with his wife. When he arrived home after the meeting, he was so full of joy that his wife thought he had been drinking so she telephoned the chapter president's wife for an explanation. Such was the transformation in her husband's life that she willingly came along to the next dinner meeting to see for herself what God can do.

Travelling through Sussex one day, David stopped to ask directions at a small antiques' shop at a cross-roads. When someone did him a service he would always give them a *Voice* magazine as a way of saying thank you, and he did so on this occasion. As he was about to drive away, the shop owner shouted out, 'You are two weeks too late.' David went back into the shop to find out what she meant. On the cover of that particular edition were the words: 'Two Weeks Saved My Marriage.' The lady told David she was desperately unhappy because her husband had just gone off with another woman. He prayed with her and gave her the address of the local FGBMFI chapter. Her parting comment was, 'You were not here by chance this morning. God sent you.'

On one occasion the Lord used *Voice* as a matchmaker! Buzz Dulley, father of three grown-up daughters, had lost his wife from cancer and he wrote his testimony for *Voice* magazine. It was then published in American *Voice* in January 1982, and a lady called Jo whose senator husband had died, leaving her with four grown-up sons, read his story. Jo had a friend who needed to know more about baptism in the Holy Spirit, so she wrote to Buzz to ask if he would write to this lady. Buzz didn't do anything for four months, but in July that year he was going to the world convention in Anaheim, California, and before he went he decided to get his correspondence up to date. He wrote to Jo's friend and then to her saying he had done what she asked. After the first meeting of the convention, Buzz decided to go into the coffee shop where he was greeted by a friend. Hearing his name, a lady tapped him on the shoulder and said, 'You must be that Englishman? I'm Jo who wrote to you.' Jo then asked Buzz if he would record his testimony on tape for her to use on a radio programme.

In February of the following year, Jo wrote to Buzz again saying that the sound quality of the tape was so poor she was unable to use it but if he was going to the Detroit convention that summer, perhaps they could retape the interview. Buzz did not really want to go and prayed that the Lord would give him two good reasons for going. Shortly afterwards he received a telephone call from Bill Cooke, a Field Representative in Ohio, who asked if he would come and speak at some of the chapters in Ohio following the convention. Decided that he now had two good reasons to go, Buzz made his booking. He arranged to meet Jo to redo the interview but she was so nervous that she forgot to switch the machine on. By the second day of the convention they realised that they had fallen in love! Although Buzz didn't ask her to marry him, within three days he knew they would get married. They decided on a wedding at Thanksgiving but early one morning God woke Buzz up and said, 'What are you waiting for? This is my marriage. Get on with it.' Buzz phoned Jo and told her that God had said they must not delay. He asked her to fix everything up for Saturday week—it was then Tuesday! At their wedding 200 guests were present although not a single invitation had been given out. There were no gifts, people just brought something along to eat and someone baked a four-tier wedding cake. Buzz and Jo learned much about trusting God totally as obstacles in such a short time of preparation melted away.

Jo had never been to England before. She left four sons, two cars, a home and grandchildren, as well as a very good job, but she had absolute peace that it was God's will. For Buzz, one of the remarkable things was that he had been a widower for twelve years and had never given a thought to marrying again. However, in the months before the Detroit convention, four FGBMFI men had said to him, 'How about getting married again?' One of the things Buzz packed when going to Detroit was a tie which he only wore at weddings, and he had no idea why he took it with him! Over the last four years God has used Buzz and Jo to travel all over the world, spreading the Gospel, encouraging chapters and seeing God move in power.

One last testimony regarding *Voice*. Bob Preston, now a member of the Wakefield chapter, was a driver for Mercedes Benz and his boss, Dudley Jackson, was President of the Bradford chapter. Dudley frequently passed

Voice magazines to Bob which he promptly threw away without reading. One day his little girl came home from Sunday school and told him the vicar wanted to see him in church that Tuesday. His first reaction was 'No way' but then he realised he was doing what his parents had done—sending their child to Sunday school but never setting foot inside the church themselves. He and his wife went along that night and were surprised by the crowds going in. There were so many people that car-park attendants were needed. He had never remembered church being like that. The following morning he was driving a lorry up the A19 to Stockton-on-Tees when a *Voice* magazine slid over in front of him. He was about to throw it away as usual but instead found himself pulling into a lay-by. As he read through the testimonies he knew that he needed to find Jesus in the same way, and there and then in his cab he asked Jesus to come and take over his life.

When he got back to the office Bob told Dudley what he had done and there was great excitement. Dudley invited Bob and his wife to the next Bradford breakfast where he was baptised in the Holy Spirit and she was healed of a kidney complaint. Giving his testimony in the Hull one-day convention in April 1986, Bob told how someone said that he couldn't have been baptised in the Holy Spirit as he was not speaking in tongues. Bob was so concerned that he arranged for his wife and himself to talk with Bert and Pauline Sture in their home. They talked about their faith for two hours and then prayed. As Bob was driving down into Bradford, he turned to his wife to ask her what she thought of all they'd heard but he found himself speaking in tongues. Every time he opened his mouth he began to speak in a language he had never learned, so he drove with one hand on the steering-wheel and the other over his mouth. At the end of his testimony, Bob told everybody how much fun he had had since becoming a Christian and how he praised God that he, too, was one of 'the happiest people on earth'.

There is no doubt that God has used not only the American and European editions of *Voice*, but also the story of Demos Shakarian and the beginnings of the FGBMFI. David Daw, now at Bible school in the United States but formerly a Field Representative and President of the Southport chapter, first came into contact with the Fellowship in the late 1950s. His father's friend emigrated to the United States and sent them various Christian magazines, including one with Billy Graham on the cover, called *Voice*. Then in 1966, when some of the Americans came over for the chartering of the Lancashire chapter, Walter Moore came to speak at the church David attended and he was baptised in the Holy Spirit. He then met Allan Jones, who came to know the Lord after coming into contact with friends at his church, and in the early 1970s joined the Preston chapter. Although he read the *Voice* magazines and news letters, he was a member for six years before he went to a dinner.

Just before Christmas 1977, David's brother rang him to say he had read a marvellous book called *The Happiest People on Earth*. David drove into Southport in order to buy a copy but couldn't find anywhere to park, so feeling very frustrated he started to drive back home. Suddenly he saw Allan Jones coming out of a shop and pulled up to talk to him. David explained that he had been into town because he wanted a particular book but had not been able to park anywhere. Allan said, 'Never mind, I've got a boot full of a book that's just been published. I'll give you a copy to read over Christmas.' When Allan opened the car boot and David saw there all the copies of *The Happiest People on Earth*, he knew God had arranged this meeting. He could not put the book down and, inspired by the vision of what the Fellowship was about, he began to work towards his vision for a chapter in Southport. Shortly after this he went to his first dinner meeting at Preston. The speaker was from the United States—he was Walter Moore!

The story of Bernard Deniel, involved in running a young peoples' outdoor centre in the Pickering area, again shows how God can use inspired Christian literature. Bernard was walking through Malton one Saturday morning when he passed the church of St Michael's. At that time he was feeling very low mentally and physically, and something prompted him to go back and enter the church. He sat down in a pew and for the first time in many years, felt at peace. God had been speaking to him for a long time to do something with his life, but he constantly put it off until a more convenient time. After sitting for a while, he began to potter round the church and look at the windows but was then drawn to the bookstall. There was a tremendous variety of colourful books and pamphlets but his eyes kept going to one particular cover. It was fairly plain in design, with a white background and the title picked out in bright colours: *The Happiest People on Earth*.

Bernard left the money, took the book home with him, and began to read it. His first reaction was 'I don't believe this. It can't be true'. But deep down inside he wanted to believe it, he knew it was what he had been searching for, but somehow it was all too much. He put the book to one side with a pile of others and left it for about a year. Then one day he picked it up again, took it to bed that night and read it right through. He read it again and again and again—seven times in all. To make sure he had really grasped it, he then began to read it out loud to himself. He knew he had to find out more about this Fellowship and wrote off to the address given. Bernard discovered there was a chapter almost on his doorstep and arranged to go to a dinner meeting.

At the dinner, Bernard explained to Geoff Woods, the President, how he had come to be there and Geoff asked if he would tell the others how God had changed his life through reading that book. David and I had the privilege of praying for him at the end of the meeting and the Lord touched him in such a way that he could not stop laughing. Since then he has been a marvellous witness for the Lord and has become a stalwart member of the chapter.

The Psalmist says, 'Has the Lord redeemed you? Then speak it out!' (Ps 107:2, The Living Bible). The stories concerning *Voice* and *The Happiest People on Earth* clearly show how God is able to use the testimonies of ordinary men and women. A delightful quote from Canon Alan Glendinning, Chaplain to the Queen and former Rector of Sandringham, best sums it up. Speaking to John Wright on one occasion he said, 'John, testimony is the most ancient and scriptural form of evangelism. St Paul was always at it!'

13

Come Over And Help Us

Making the Full Gospel Business Men's Fellowship 'International' has always been in the minds of the founder and leaders since its inception. Initially, that outreach was done by the Americans themselves, going into Canada, South America, Asia, Europe and, of course, the United Kingdom and Ireland. In this country, we owe a great debt to those men who gave so willingly of their time and finance to bring the vision of the Fellowship to us. Now the men of the United Kingdom and Ireland have taken up the mantle of outreach into Europe and Africa.

Late in 1979 a decision was taken to set up a European Advisory Council to take responsibility for the oversight of the FGBMFI work in Europe. Coincidental with that decision came the announcement that Steve Lightle would be leaving Europe to undertake a work in Israel and Jim Guhlke of the Brussels office would be returning to Seattle. Following this news David Molyneux was appointed Acting Director of the Brussels office and Bob Spilman, as well as being International Director for the United Kingdom and Ireland, was appointed as European Chapter and Convention Co-ordinator. This council has a representative from each country in Europe where FGBMFI is working, and they seek to be led by the Holy Spirit in expanding the work of the Fellowship. Members of the Fellowship are encouraged to move out into countries as they feel led by the Spirit.

Men are not specially chosen for this task. Sometimes they may be asked by a director, but more often a general appeal will be given when an airlift is arranged, or individuals or chapters will organise their own outreach. It should be stressed here that this travelling is usually done at the individual's expense and is not in general funded by the Fellowship.

Between 1976 and the setting up of the Council in 1979, Steve Lightle travelled many thousands of miles by car in West and East Europe, as a matter of policy, always accompanied by another member of the Fellowship. While in Hungary he saw the possibility of having an FGBMFI convention and discussed the matter with church leaders and officials. It was agreed that FGBMFI could have the use of a large convention hall in Budapest and arrangements were made for an airlift to take place in October 1978.

Steve needed to finalise the arrangements in Budapest but had no one to travel with him. He prayed about whom he should ask and it was a very surprised Bob Spilman who received a phone call from Steve, then in Switzerland, asking if Bob would meet him in Budapest. Bob, who at that time had no experience of travelling in Eastern Europe, said he would be prepared to go to Budapest but didn't have the necessary funds. Steve and Bob prayed together over the phone for the release of the funds. The following morning a cheque arrived in the post from the London chapter paying for the air ticket and a few days' stay in Hungary. A note with the cheque said the chapter was moved to send this because they felt that Bob should go to Hungary. The members had no knowledge of the immediate need. Steve and Bob met at Budapest airport and then met with a number of officials who were very eager for a group of businessmen to come to their country. Most of those who attended were from the United States, but there were others from the United Kingdom and West Germany. About sixty people came in all, including Demos and Rose Shakarian and Tommy Ashcraft.

About one week prior to the convention, the authorities contacted Steve Lightle to cancel the arrangements for use of the convention hall because they had not realised they were Christian businessmen and that the meeting was intended to be a Christian gathering. By this time it was too late to stop the people on the airlift from travelling as they had already paid for tickets and so they arrived in Budapest on 2nd October 1978 and were accommodated in the Hilton Hotel.

In the evening while the group was eating, a messenger came to say that a large crowd was gathering outside the hotel and wanted to meet with Demos and the people from the airlift. Many of those who were gathering had come from other East European countries, including Poland, Czechoslovakia, Romania, Bulgaria and East Germany. They refused to disperse so Demos and others were allowed to speak to them. There followed the first FGBMFI 'street meeting' and as a result some came to a saving knowledge of Jesus, others were healed, and still others were baptised in the Holy Spirit. The ministry continued in the hotel bedrooms.

As the convention hall was not available, the people from the airlift had to meet in churches and so at very short notice arrangements were made to transport small groups to different places in the city of Budapest and also to many different parts of Hungary. This continued for the remainder of the week and everyone was encouraged at the power of God demonstrated in the meetings.

At one packed meeting in a church, time was very limited as the church had to be shut for the night very early. Demos only spoke for eight minutes and then the Holy Spirit moved in the congregation to heal the sick. Following this a call for salvation led to a very large response from all over the church. One young boy who was almost completely deaf was prayed for and was healed. The following day the father came to the hotel and gave his heart and life to Jesus.

Bob Spilman went with one group of seven to Lake Balatou. Many healings took place after the teaching as the people were so receptive. One young woman who had been involved in the occult needed deliverance. At first the demons refused to leave her, but they had no alternative when confronted by those who had faith in the name of Jesus and the power of his blood. The young woman was set free only just in time for those praying for her to catch the mini-bus back to Budapest. Physically released, she was a changed person as she waved goodbye. Every group had an exciting tale to tell and it was here that contacts were also made for future work in Poland.

Bob and Millicent Spilman have visited Poland along with other men of the Fellowship as God has opened the doors. Ted Collier, who has worked in the Field Office on a voluntary basis for some years, was one of those who went to Poland. Bob went into the Field Office one morning in September 1984 and told Ted that he had been praying about Poland the previous night and his name and that of his wife, Pam, had come into his mind. When Ted came to know the Lord at the age of fifty-three, he had begun to travel and became excited by it. He went home and told Pam what Bob had said and her immediate reaction was that they should pray about it. While praying the Lord gave them a verse, Ezekiel 3 verse 11, and when they read the words they knew it was confirmation: 'Go now to your countrymen in exile and speak to them. Say to them, "This is what the Sovereign Lord says," whether they listen or fail to listen' (NIV). When Ted looked up the cross references with that scripture he read, 'Do not be afraid of their words or their looks.'

Apart from the drabness of the country, what impressed Ted most was the immense desire on the part of the Christians to receive from the Lord. Their first meeting was to be a teaching session in a hotel. When they went in, the room looked more like a classroom with everyone sitting at desks, pencils and notebooks at the ready. After the morning session, the people were prayed for and a girl received the baptism of the Holy Spirit. During the time of ministry in the evening meeting, she began shouting and crying and Ted thought she had 'gone over the top'. However, Pam told him they had prayed for her and her eyesight had been healed. Immediately after that meeting she had to rush to get a train back to East Germany where she worked but where she had no Christian Fellowship.

At the Presidents' and Officers' weekend in Blackpool, in February 1987, Bob Spilman appealed for men to go to countries like Poland. He told them that Western Christians are so privileged it is almost impossible to comprehend the desperate spiritual needs of those behind the 'iron curtain'.

Hungary is another Eastern European country which God has opened up to the Fellowship. At the Brussels convention in 1983, Jim Winter was chairman of the Saturday morning breakfast meeting. Walking out of the room at the close of the meeting, he was stopped by an Englishman called David Hathaway who knew a great deal about the issue of Christianity in iron-curtain countries. He asked Jim if he had ever thought of starting the Fellowship behind the iron curtain, particularly in Hungary. Jim said he hadn't but would pray about it and

David replied that he would contact him at a later date. By now Jim was an International Director and was already travelling in Europe, so he needed to be sure that the Hungary project was right for him. While praying one day, he asked the Lord to direct him in some way and turned to Acts chapter 16 where Paul received a vision of a man from Macedonia standing and begging him, 'Come over to Macedonia and help us' (Acts 16:9, NIV). Jim told the Lord he was willing to go but asked that when he spoke to the men in Hungary, they would say that they gave him the Macedonian call.

When Jim's plane landed at the airport in Hungary, he was met by John and an interpreter, Erica. As they travelled along in the car, John said something to Erica in Hungarian and she turned to Jim and said, 'Brother, John has just told me to tell you this: the brothers in Hungary give you a Macedonian call.' Jim could only sit and weep at the way God had moved. He had not been able to say for certain that he would make that particular trip, but the Hungarian Christians with whom he had contact felt a complete assurance in their hearts that he would. This was demonstrated when they made their first stop. It was at the building site of a new Pentecostal church just outside Budapest, and the ceremony for laying the foundation stone was about to take place. Underneath the foundation they were burying some artefacts for posterity, including a scroll which was read out for Jim: 'We would like to thank FGBMFI for their work with us and help to us for this country and we personally thank brother Jim Winter for coming over to be with us at this ceremony.' This was truly 'faith in action'. Jim felt as if he were walking along a path of destiny.

In Hungary a religious organisation is not permitted outside of the church, which is the only 'institution' accepted by the authorities. Because of this, the government has classed FGBMFI with the Pentecostals. This is not due to any wish on the part of the Fellowship, it was an administrative decision at government level. God had everything in hand, for the Fellowship needed an office, and the Pentecostal church outside Budapest, where Jim had been at the stone-laying ceremony, provided this office. By paying five years' rent in advance, the FGBMFI were able to contribute to the building of that church.

One of the greatest needs of the Christians in Hungary is transport. At the men's 'advance' in Scotland in October 1984, money was given for a mini-bus for the work of the Fellowship in Hungary. Jim went over in July 1986 with the money given at the Scottish advance and as much again donated by the Brussels office. His intention was to buy the vehicle in Hungary, but he was told there was nothing in the country and he would have to wait at least six to twelve months. Officials wanted Jim to bank the money in Hungary but he was not prepared to do that. Eventually he was able to buy a second-hand minibus, complete with a spare set of tyres (more precious than gold in that country), and still have enough to pay the 50% tax on whatever value the government put on the bus—such items are usually well overvalued. If they had bought a new vehicle, the tax rate would have been 100%. What a wonderful day it was in August 1986 when Jim drove the bus and handed it over to the FGBMFI in Hungary where there are now ten groups of men, each one numbering between four and twenty-five.

For most of his time in Hungary, Jim has travelled on his own, but on 4th April 1986, Hungarian National Day of Liberation, he arrived with two other men, Duncan Dougall, President of the Stirling/Falkirk chapter, and Don McHutchon, Vice-President of the Lanarkshire chapter. They were met by John, now the national leader of the FGBMFI, who had arranged for them to speak at nine different meetings in ten days. During that visit they were allowed to travel extensively in the country without any difficulties and it became evident that the Lord had prepared the way before them. On their second day they were introduced to a group of gypsies who were on fire for the Lord and who had a great longing to reach their people for Jesus. At their first meeting with them, five gypsies committed their lives to Jesus and an invitation was extended to the men to go to another part of the country on their next trip.

In the North of the country, the group of believers they met with told them they had been praying specifically for their visit for three weeks. So it was not surprising that the Holy Spirit came down upon those meetings in great power and many were saved, healed and baptised in the Holy Spirit. Towards the end of their visit, they met some top people in the Hungarian film industry who were making a social documentary film concerned with the increase in such things as solvent abuse and the disruption of the family in Hungary. While preparing to film, they had come across a group of Christians who had found an answer to these problems and who greatly impressed them. The film-makers watched this group of believers build a church complex from scratch in only six months. They filmed extensively in the church, telling the story of one young man who had been bound in rebellion and violence, but after coming to know the Lord, was free to sing and praise God. The producer was hoping that the film would be shown in schools throughout Hungary. What excited the three men from Scotland was when they realised the church complex was the one in which the FGBMFI had its office and that God was moving there in a mighty way.

May 1987 saw the first outreach to North-east Yugoslavia when two Englishmen, Peter Ashburner from Northwich and Ken Eaves from Liverpool, teamed up with two Americans. The report of that visit was described as reading like a chapter from the Acts of the Apostles. They left Belgrade and drove a hired car down to Subotica, near the Romanian and Hungarian borders, where they had the name, address and telephone number of a contact. This man, Victor Sabo, is the Assistant Pastor of a Pentecostal church and an Area Secretary, and he was also able to interpret for them.

Victor knew about the FGBMFI after a contact in 1983 with a team from Alberta and he had also met Demos Shakarian in Berlin. He had planned a series of meetings for the men in his area. The meetings were small but each time they experienced a powerful anointing of the Holy Spirit. During the ministry time in one meeting, two people received salvation, one the baptism of the Holy Spirit, and a number were healed. The pastor's back was healed, and one person was healed of arthritis and another of rheumatism. Yet another person's ear was healed, sinus problems vanished, and evil spirits were cast out. Each person prayed for received instant healing and this was thrilling both for the team and the congregation. That particular evening they received a word of encouragement from the Lord saying that if they gave him the glory they would see even greater things as he moved through them by his Spirit. The Lord also went on to say, 'Do not be afraid because I am with you, my hand is stretched out to save and to heal and in my name the demons must flee.'

In every place they visited, people were saved, set free and healed, as well as baptised in the Holy Spirit. It was a memorable visit for each member of the team where they not only had the opportunity of ministering but were also ministered to by the people. They were overwhelmed by the love and friendliness shown to them and the way the people provided food after every meeting. Not only were they able to share the vision of the FGBMFI in theory, but also in practice, and in every town at least one man grasped hold of what the Fellowship was all about. The men from the FGBMFI are trusting God that they will be able to return with others to build on the foundations laid.

Allan Jones was in a leaders' meeting in Belgium when Spiros Patisas spoke about the needs in Greece. Feeling a leap in his spirit, Allan asked the Lord to confirm if he was to go and once again came those words from Acts chapter 16 regarding the man from Macedonia who asked Paul to 'come over and help us'. Allan has seen the Lord move in some dramatic ways in Greece. On one occasion, when giving out *Voice* magazines in Athens with Roger Sharpe from Kent, he spoke to a young drug addict who told them he was going to commit suicide. After sharing what Jesus can do, Allan and Roger prayed about the drug problem and this young man fell over under the power of the Spirit.

On one occasion he was invited to speak in a church in Thessalonica and a young lady was asked to interpret for him. She told how on the previous day she had had a dream that she was in church translating from English to Greek. Neither she nor anyone else knew at that stage that Allan was going to be there, but God knew. In February 1987 Allan went out with Roger Sharp and Steve Dobbins from the States to inaugurate the second FGBMFI chapter in Athens. As the men went to a member's flat, they saw a young man and the Holy Spirit told Allan that he needed prayer for his legs. As he was prayed for he was immediately healed. Hearing the excitement, the parents of the young man came out of their apartment and all three gave their lives to Jesus. At a chapter meeting at which about 200 were present, this young man shared his new-found faith.

In a restaurant later that same evening, the Holy Spirit again prompted them that one of the Greek men at an adjacent table had a back problem. Allan went to pray for him and he was healed. As a result of this miracle he and six companions gave their lives to Jesus.

The impetus for a work of the Fellowship in Portugal came in a most unexpected way. A Portuguese seaman, Emmanuel Alves, went to Sunderland Marine and Technology College for a period of study, and one of his lecturers was a friend of Albert Hodgson, President of the Northumbria chapter. This friend invited Emmanuel to his church on Seamen's Sunday, but apparently Emmanuel was not too impressed so a phone call was made to Albert to see if he would take this Portuguese gentleman to a livelier meeting in the evening. Albert took him along to church and Emmanuel was filled with the Holy Spirit and attended an FGBMFI breakfast meeting the following Saturday.

What amused Albert about Emmanuel was that he joined the chapter, paid his annual membership fee more promptly than anyone, and yet was the most infrequent attender. The problem was that most of the time he was away at sea, but whenever he could he would fly over to have fellowship. He was so enthusiastic about the Fellowship that he kept asking when they were going to move into Portugal. After visiting America, he visited Bob Spilman on New Year's Eve 1984 saying, 'When are you going to start chapters in Portugal, and when are you going to print *Voice* and *The Happiest People on Earth* in Portuguese?' The following spring, with support from David Wells, International Director from New England, Bob Spilman and Millicent, together with some other American and French men and women, four men from the Warrington chapter—David and Frank Antrobus, Colin Pownall and Lucio Soccorro—and Iain Ogilvie from the Wirral chapter, met together in Lisbon.

They visited the Portuguese towns of Faro and Altura as well as the Spanish town of Huelva, submitting to the Lord's guidance on their course of action in each case.

As in all outreaches, these were ordinary men who were quite inexperienced in this kind of work, and going in 'cold' meant they had to rely totally on the Lord for every need. They later shared that the most vital part of that outreach was the corporate prayer life of the group, together with intercessory prayer from those at home.

In Altura they met a Spanish pastor who had worked for fifteen years in the town, caring for the needs of a number of small churches and praying constantly for a real visitation of the Holy Spirit. During the morning of the team's first day in that town, words of encouragement came from the Lord, together with a realisation that they were to be engaged in spiritual warfare in this town where there was much superstition and many occult practices. At the evening meeting many people were healed and baptised in the Holy Spirit, so they decided to stay a further night contrary to previous plans. There were about 100 people in the congregation at the second evening meeting and 80 came forward to receive baptism in the Holy Spirit. Many of these, and others, were healed and the ministry did not finish until after midnight. On returning to their hotel, some of the team went into a late-night bar to talk with young people, many of whom were on drugs. Meanwhile the rest of the team interceded in prayer at the hotel. Six young people came to know Jesus that night.

Having travelled into Spain, the team returned to Lisbon where they met again with others from the United Kingdom and America. They decided to go into Liberty Avenue where they talked to male prostitutes. The power of the Gospel led to tears of repentance. One young transvestite went home, removed his make-up and woman's clothes, dressed as a man, and returned to the street to share his new-found faith. That night over twenty people gave their lives to Christ, including an inquisitive policeman who had simply stopped to investigate what was happening!

Once these initial outreaches have taken place, there is a need to build upon the work done. As Dillon Harris puts it, after the initial impact, the situation looks as if someone has thrown in a hand-grenade. Then the Holy Spirit, whose work it is, enables men to go back and encourage those who have been contacted so that over a period of time relationships are built up and chapters established.

Sometimes a team of men may be invited to a country which already has well-established chapters, but for various reasons are experiencing difficulties and need encouragement and support. Such was the case in Norway. Bert Sture, International Director from Bradford, is of Norwegian extraction and, along with others in the North-East region, has long had a concern for Norway. While there are times when men find themselves abroad within two or three weeks of the invitation being extended, the vision of a team going to Norway took a number of years to come to fruition.

At the Wembley convention in 1980, Don Ostrom asked men if they were prepared to go to Europe, telling them to return home, get a passport and be ready. My husband, David, did just that, and prayed that the Lord would show him where he must go. About four years later, as he was praying, he saw himself and Bert Sture ministering together in Norway. It wasn't until September 1987 that that vision was realised. David and Bert, along with Peter Sutherland, a former stockbroker from Singapore but now returned to Grimsby, and Cecil Mather, an administrator in the meat industry from Northern Ireland, set off for a fifteen-day journey round Norway and Sweden.

Their boat docked in Bergen on Sunday afternoon and they were met by the local President, Rolf, who said, 'You have come just at the right time. The devil has been trying to destroy this chapter.' In their hotel room, within half an hour of their arrival, he rededicated his life to the Lord and received a tremendously encouraging word of prophecy: 'Forget the past—you serve an "I am" God.' The Bergen chapter had been helped for six months by Victor Smith from Sierra Leone, a man whom the Lord used greatly. God spoke to him and said he would send other men to Bergen after he left, 'This is the promise,' said Rolf, 'fulfilled today.'

After their first chapter meeting that Sunday night (the churches do not have Sunday evening services) when the Lord ministered to the people, they were invited to take part in a live radio programme. *GODT NGTT* (Good News) Radio Bergen goes out once a month at midnight on Sunday and reaches about 50,000 listeners. It is organised by the FGBMFI and after testimonies are shared, people are invited to phone in to the programme. This is another example of God's perfect timing, because originally they were not going to be in Bergen that night, but the itinerary had to be changed. God used their testimonies to speak to people and so many calls came in that they were able to pray over the air with those in need.

The second evening they visited Haugesund. When it came to the ministry time, no one moved. Then the Lord gave David a word that there were people with back problems who needed to be healed. In any meeting one can expect a number of people with back ailments, but when that word was given, nearly thirty out of the fifty people present responded. It was the key to what became a very powerful time of ministry. They visited seven chapters in Norway and the Lord used them to challenge the members to return to the vision of the Fellowship: bringing unsaved men and women to hear how God can change their lives. A lot of time on this visit to Norway was spent in encouraging others, and bringing healing and deliverance in the power of the Holy Spirit.

While in Jonkoping, Sweden, they visited the home of Per Ariel and his wife, Marianne. He took them to the hospital to visit Lars, the son of a friend, who was recovering from an attempted suicide. They talked and prayed with him but there was little apparent response, and he remained very confused. However, in the next bed was a ninety-two-year-old man who wanted to know what was going on. Per explained that these men had been praying that Jesus would heal Lars and he was so intrigued, he wanted to know more. At the end of the conversation, this old man asked Jesus to come into his life.

One very touching incident happened while in Norway. The weekend in the middle of the itinerary was spent in a log cabin in the middle of a forest. The President, whose company owned a number of these cabins, invited a Norwegian family and also an English family who lived out there to look after the men for the weekend. The English couple had three children and their middle daughter had just had her tenth birthday. Before the four men left she came to them and said she had been given 35 Krone in birthday money and she wanted to give her tithe of 3.5 Krone to help towards their expenses. What a blessing that gift was and what a testimony to parents who were bringing up their children in the ways of the Lord.

Don Latham has had the opportunity of going over to France to visit the chapters there and speak at a men's weekend. At the latter event, he was speaking on how to receive answers to prayer and during the meeting the Lord gave him a picture of all these men falling under the power of the Spirit. The Lord said, 'All you have to do is to speak my name.' When it came to the ministry time, Don asked men who wanted the Lord's anointing to receive answers to their prayers to come out and for others to stand behind them. Every man there stood up, so Don called them out in thirties, lined them up and went along the line saying, 'In the name of Jesus.' After twenty minutes, apart from the six leaders, every single man was on the floor. Then the Lord gave him a word of prophecy for the leaders and each one of them fell under the power of the Holy Spirit. Such was the power of God that as those six men stood with Don, they could feel a tremendous heat even though the temperature in the rest of the room remained the same.

There are so many testimonies of what God has done when men have gone out in his name that it is impossible to cover them all here. God has opened up doors in Malta, Morocco, Egypt, Burkino Faso, Liberia, the Ivory Coast, and there are many more countries where contacts have been made. One last example shows how God uses the most unexpected people to act as a link in his developing pattern.

Geoffrey Peters is an ex-businessman from Peshawar in Pakistan, a North-West frontier province. In 1985 he was studying theology at Oakhill Theological College. He was invited to the Finchley chapter and came forward for prayer after hearing Allan Jones share his testimony. Geoffrey had seen people falling down under the power of the Spirit but did not want it to happen to him. God has his way of dealing with such resistance, and he found himself lying on the floor. As he was lying there he had a vision of himself speaking in a language which was totally unknown to him, despite the fact that he speaks six different languages. He went home after the meeting, not aware of what had happened but realising that God had touched him. One of his problems was sitting down to write essays, but as soon as he got home he sat down, worked right through the night and, to the delight of his tutors, produced one of his best essays to date. He then told his tutors about his experience at the dinner and they were able to confirm to him that he had been baptised in the Holy Spirit.

Three months later, the Anglican Bishop of Peshawar was in London and Geoffrey took him along to the Finchley chapter. He was so encouraged by seeing businessmen sharing the truth with other businessmen that when he got back to Peshawar he contacted Geoffrey's brother and together they were able to gather a group of men and form the first chapter in Pakistan.

Listening to the accounts of men from the Fellowship who have visited other countries, one common factor emerges. There is no surer way of enthusing men for God than giving them the opportunity of fulfilling the great commission; to go into all the world and preach the Gospel, and to see signs and wonders done in the name of Jesus.

Epilogue

'We've come this far by faith' sang the five young ex-drug addicts that Saturday morning of 20th November 1965, as they were waiting to board the plane at Los Angeles International Airport. We do not have a record of their names, but that does not matter. The important thing is that they, along with the other men and women, had caught the vision of what God wanted for their lives: to share the good news of the Gospel of Jesus Christ.

For the majority of those taking part in the airlift it was a step of faith, not only in a spiritual but also a financial sense. They were just ordinary men and women marked out by one important fact—they had made themselves available to God. And that is the story of the Full Gospel Business Men's Fellowship International in the United Kingdom and Ireland. Without exception they are all ordinary men and women with no special talents or abilities whom God has used to bring the Fellowship 'this far by faith'.

I wonder if any of those Christians, from different parts of the United States and from a wide variety of church and cultural backgrounds, had any conception that morning of what was beginning. I trust that many of them will read what God has been able to accomplish because of their faithfulness.

The stories of men such as Bill Thompson, John Walker, Bob Spilman, John Wright and David Rose, to name but a few, are testimonies of how God can take an ordinary individual, change his life around and use him in his service. As mentioned before, these men are all like the Apostle Paul, still 'pressing on towards the prize'. Problems and difficulties still intrude upon their lives, but they have learned that 'in all things we are more than conquerors through Him who loved us' (Rom 8:37).

Back in 1965, Ray Barnett's vision had been for a convention in London which would reach thousands of people with the Gospel. In bringing that to pass God was also bringing to reality the vision he gave to Demos Shakarian in December 1952 of men all over the world, transformed by the love of God and set free, standing shoulder to shoulder with heads and arms raised towards heaven.

How far has the FGBMFI in this country kept faithful to that vision? I believe that for many of the men involved, the vision is as real as if it had been given to them personally. The Fellowship has been faithful in seeking to implement that vision. At times it has been necessary to call the men of the chapters together to 'Get Back to Basics'—the theme of the men's weekend in Blackpool in February 1987. In being faithful they have been successful.

The Fellowship in the United Kingdom and Ireland is now growing faster than almost anywhere in the world. God is using ordinary men to reach out into Europe and Africa, taking over the baton, as it were, in their part of the race to enable others to 'catch the vision' and lift up the name of Jesus so that all men may be drawn to him.

Appendix 1: Letter from the Reverend John Stride

California has produced more religious cranks, oddball organisations and curious cults than anywhere else in the world. So it is not surprising that I should have misgivings when I came across an organisation founded by an Armenian Pentecostal dairy farmer in California. With an origin like that, a name like 'Full Gospel Business Men's Fellowship International', and a record of rapid growth around the world, it hardly looked the sort of thing that a Church of England vicar in rural Norfolk would want to get involved in.

What's more, there seemed to be so many good reasons for not giving it more than a passing thought. The name itself was enough to put you off.

'Full Gospel'—well, we Anglicans have got the full Gospel. We don't claim to have a monopoly of the truth, but you would have to go a long way to find a better summary of the good news than the thirty-nine Articles. So what can the FGBMFI add? Why should we need it?

'Fellowship'—now, there's a dangerous word. A fellowship group in the church is fine. But can I encourage people to spend their precious spare time, or mine, in a group which isn't directly connected with the church? After all, our small village churches need all the help they can get.

'International'—that simply means that it is American and things American are suspect. There are still plenty in Norfolk whose attitude to America and things American is summed up in the old complaint about US servicemen in World War Two. 'They're overpaid, overfed, oversexed and over here.'

Hardly a promising beginning. Perhaps the best the local FGBMFI leaders could hope for from someone like me was that I should follow Gamaliel's example: that I should not oppose the Fellowship but wait and see whether it was of God. That is probably what I would have done had not the offer of a free meal won me over. In the event my wife, Maureen, and I attended one of the first dinners of the Dereham chapter. That was nearly two years ago and in the succeeding months my misgivings were sufficiently overcome for me to become a member of the Fellowship, albeit through the generosity of one of the national leaders. But I paid my own subscription this year and shall go on doing so, and that is a true test of the value I place on the FGBMFI.

Let me go back and see if I can explain what happened to those misgivings and show how the name of the FGBMFI can be seen in a very different light.

'Full Gospel'—no, the Church of England does not fall down here. But what I found in the FGBMFI was an expectation that God would meet spiritual, physical and material needs. What I had always believed in theory was being put into practice in the Fellowship. Like the Church of England at large, I began to rediscover the ministry of healing and other gifts of the Spirit.

'Business men'—our churches have not been overwhelmed by an influx of men through the ministry of FGBMFI, at least not yet. But the Fellowship is by no means a sort of Christian version of free-masonry. The men whom I have taken to dinners have been blessed and have grown in their faith as a result, as have I. But it is among the women who have attended dinners that the most dramatic and exciting changes have taken place. Seeing people saved, transformed and delighting in God, as we have at the FGBMFI, is a wonderful thing. Not the least of the benefits to the life of our churches has been the increased willingness and desire of people to talk about their faith and the Lord because of the example they have been given at the FGBMFI.

'Fellowship'—I have found it enriching to share the good news with men from all denominations and all sorts of backgrounds; men who are bound together by a bond that transcends all barriers, and have a common desire to serve the Lord in the power of the Holy Spirit. The FGBMFI says that it exists to serve the churches and I have found that to be no idle boast. Certainly in the Dereham chapter there is a real awareness of the danger of drawing people's energy away from the churches. I think that the best indication of their attitude is the statement made whenever a collection is taken at a dinner. We are always told, 'Don't give anything to the Fellowship that you would normally give to your church', and they are not just talking about money. I have found that my involvement in the FGBMFI has only added to, and never detracted from, the life of the churches for which I am responsible.

'International'—well, what's wrong with success? The Fellowship has grown from a single group in suburban California to over 4,000 chapters in ninety-three countries within thirty-five years. In itself that is no recommendation because weeds grow faster than flowers. But the FGBMFI is not a weed in the spiritual garden. In fact, I believe that the FGBMFI has been raised up by God as one of the means he intends to use to meet the needs of our age. My reasons are these. First that the stance of the Fellowship is both biblical and expectant. Anyone who believes that the Bible is to be taken as God's authoritative word for today, and that the Holy Spirit is at work in the world today, just as he was in the time of the Apostles, can be a part of the Fellowship. There is no denying that God is blessing the way in which the FGBMFI is bringing people of all denominations together in worship and mission. Anglicans and Baptists, Roman Catholics and Pentecostals are among those who have spoken at recent Dereham chapter dinners, sharing their experiences of the love and power of God in their everyday lives.

My second reason is that though the FGBMFI is international, its leadership is local. Each chapter is founded and led by local people who are committed to the life of local churches. Expansion is not controlled from California through some corporate plan. It takes place because ordinary Christian men want their friends and workmates to come to know Jesus and they see the FGBMFI as one means that God can use to achieve that aim. After all, what better setting could there be for hearing the good news than a comfortable (modestly priced) hotel restaurant? And who better to share the good news than a working man speaking out of his own experience of God?

Could the FGBMFI play a part in the life of your church? I don't know, and it would be presumptuous of me to try to tell you. All I can do is commend it as a fellowship which God is using in our time and in our land. At the heart of the FGBMFI's philosophy is the role of personal testimony. My personal testimony is that for myself, my wife and upwards of a dozen of my parishioners, the local chapter of the Full Gospel Business Men's Fellowship International has been a source of encouragement, challenge and spiritual growth. We have all at last seen God at work. And some of us can never be the same again, because God has used FGBMFI dinners as the occasions when he has filled us with his Holy Spirit or made us whole or given us new power to live the Christian life.

I am grateful for that first invitation to a chapter dinner and glad that I didn't wait until I could dot every 'i' and cross every 't' with the FGBMFI before going along and discovering that God can use the vision of a Californian Armenian dairy farmer to bless and to build his church in England.

THE REVEREND JOHN STRIDE
Anglican Minister in the Dereham Group in charge of Hockering, Honingham, East and North Tuddenham.

Six Scriptural Steps to Salvation

Men and women still cry, 'What must I do to be saved?' The Bible provides a clear answer.

1. *Acknowledge*: 'For all have sinned and fall short of the glory of God' (Rom 3:23). 'God, have mercy on me, a sinner' (Lk 18:13).
2. *Repent*: 'Unless you repent, you too will all perish' (Lk 13:3). 'Repent, then, and turn to God, so that your sins may be wiped out' (Acts 3:19).
3. *Confess*: 'If we confess our sins, he is faithful and just and will forgive us our sins and purify us from all unrighteousness' (1 Jn 1:9).
4. *Forsake*: 'Let the wicked forsake his way, and the evil man his thoughts. Let him turn to the Lord . . . for he will freely pardon' (Is 55:7).
5. *Believe*: 'For God so loved the world that he gave his one and only Son, that whoever believes in him shall not perish but have eternal life' (Jn 3:16).
6. *Receive*: 'He came to that which was his own, but his own did not receive him. Yet to all who received him, to those who believed in his name, he gave the right to become children of God' (Jn 1:11–12).

Why not make your eternal decision right now? 'I am convinced by God's word that I am a lost sinner. I believe that Jesus Christ died for sinners and shed his blood to put away my sins. I now receive him as my personal Lord and Saviour and I will, by his help, confess him before men.'

When you have made this greatest of all decisions, please write to us:

NAME..

ADDRESS ....

....

....

Post to: Allan Jones, c/o Field Office—FGBMFI, PO Box 11, Knutsford, Cheshire WA16 9EB.

Outside UK: 30 Mechelse Steenweg, B-3000 Leuven, Belgium. Tel: 01032 16 207944.